that I may
LIVE
in his kingdom

DEVOTIONS BASED ON
THE NEW TRANSLATION OF
LUTHER'S SMALL CATECHISM

by Louis E. Ulrich Jr.

AUGSBURG PUBLISHING HOUSE, MINNEAPOLIS, MINN.

THAT I MAY LIVE IN HIS KINGDOM

Copyright © 1963 Augsburg Publishing House

Library of Congress Catalog Card No. 63-16605

Scripture quotations are from the Revised Standard Version of the Bible, copyright 1946 and 1952 by the Division of Christian Education of the National Council of Churches.

Sources of hymns are indicated as follows: SBH refers to *Service Book and Hymnal*, LH to *The Lutheran Hymnal*, and CSB to the *Common Service Book*.

Hymns from the *Service Book and Hymnal* of the Lutheran Church in America are used by permission of the Commission on Liturgy and Hymnal, with the following exceptions: "Praise to the Lord" (p. 11), translated by Catherine Winkworth, 1827-78, and "For the beauty of the earth" (p. 33), words by Folliott Sandford Pierpoint, 1835-1917, are used by permission of Oxford University Press, London, England; "Break thou the bread of life" (p. 193), words by Mary A. Lathbury, 1841-1913, is used by permission of the Chautauqua Institution, Chautauqua, N.Y.; "Rise up, O men of God!" (p. 102), words by William Pierson Merrill, 1867-1954, is used by permission of *The Presbyterian Outlook*, Richmond, Va.; "All creatures of our God and King" (p. 80), translated by William H. Draper, 1855-1933, and "Through the night of doubt and sorrow" (p. 205), translated by Sabine Baring-Gould, 1834-1924, are used by permission of J. Curwen and Sons, Limited, London, England.

Manufactured in the United States of America

FOREWORD

To all who have found Martin Luther's *Small Catechism* a dependable concentrate of the Gospel of Jesus Christ, I am glad to commend Pastor Ulrich's book *That I May Live in His Kingdom*. It is a devotional book for family use. The *Catechism* with Luther's explanatory material is divided to provide a text for each day in the year. The simplicity of language which Luther used and the devotional spirit in which he wrote are continued in the brief explanatory statements by Pastor Ulrich. It provides stimulus for understanding, worship and action.

FREDRIK A. SCHIOTZ
President, The American Lutheran Church

PREFACE

The original idea for a book of family devotions based on the Catechism came more than a dozen years ago from the Rev. Dr. John W. Rilling, then pastor of St. John's Lutheran church in Minneapolis, Minnesota, where I was assistant.

After his initial encouragement, I have spent hundreds of hours over the years in revising and testing the material on catechetical students and their families. The third and last complete revision had to be made last year because of the adoption of a new translation of Luther's Catechism by The American Lutheran Church, the Lutheran Church in America and the Lutheran Church—Missouri Synod. This book has been tested and revised to meet the requirements of both home and church.

I am indebted to my dear wife, who somehow managed, while taking care of a husband and five children, to do the editing and typing of the manuscript.

This book is to be used when the whole family is together, probably at the dinner table. Members of the family who are able to read well enough can take daily turns reading aloud. I suggest that one person read through an entire devotion, because the meaning and continuity are best kept that way.

After the devotion is completed as printed, where time and circumstances permit, additional Bible reading can be done, using the devotional passage as a beginning; and when a hymnal and piano are available, all the stanzas of the devotional hymn can be read or sung.

I pray that this book may help Christian families everywhere to "fight the good fight of faith."

LOUIS E. ULRICH JR.

PART ONE

The Ten Commandments

I am the Lord your God.

THE FIRST COMMANDMENT

You shall have no other gods.

> *What does this mean for us?* We are to fear, love, and trust God above anything else.

THE SECOND COMMANDMENT

You shall not take the name of the Lord your God in vain.

> *What does this mean for us?* We are to fear and love God
> so that we do not use his name
> to curse, swear, lie, or deceive,
> but call on him in prayer, praise, and
> thanksgiving.

THE THIRD COMMANDMENT

Remember the Sabbath day, to keep it holy.

> *What does this mean for us?* We are to fear and love God
> so that we do not neglect his Word
> and the preaching of it,
> but regard it as holy
> and gladly hear and learn it.

THE FOURTH COMMANDMENT

Honor your father and your mother.

What does this mean for us?

We are to fear and love God
so that we do not despise or anger our
    parents and others in authority,
but respect, obey, love, and serve them.

THE FIFTH COMMANDMENT

You shall not kill.

What does this mean for us?

We are to fear and love God
so that we do not hurt our neighbor in
    any way,
but help him in all his physical needs.

THE SIXTH COMMANDMENT

You shall not commit adultery.

What does this mean for us?

We are to fear and love God
so that in matters of sex our words and
    conduct are pure and honorable,
and husband and wife love and respect
    each other.

THE SEVENTH COMMANDMENT

You shall not steal.

What does this mean for us?

We are to fear and love God
so that we do not take our neighbor's
    money or property,
or get them in any dishonest way,
but help him to improve and protect
his property and means of making a
    living.

THE EIGHTH COMMANDMENT

You shall not bear false witness against your neighbor.

What does this mean for us?

We are to fear and love God
so that we do not betray, slander,
    or lie about our neighbor,
but defend him, speak well of him,
and explain his actions in the kindest
    way.

THE NINTH COMMANDMENT

You shall not covet your neighbor's house.

What does this mean for us?

We are to fear and love God
so that we do not desire to get our
    neighbor's possessions by scheming,
or by pretending to have a right to them,
but always help him keep what is his.

THE TENTH COMMANDMENT

You shall not covet your neighbor's wife, or his manservant, or his maidservant, or his cattle, or anything that is your neighbor's.

What does this mean for us?

We are to fear and love God
so that we do not tempt or coax away
    from our neighbor his wife or his
      workers,
but encourage them to remain loyal.

3

WHAT DOES GOD SAY OF ALL THESE COMMANDMENTS?

He says:

"I, the Lord your God, am a jealous God,
visiting the iniquity of the fathers upon the children to
the third and fourth generation of those who hate me,
but showing steadfast love to thousands of those who
love me and keep my commandments."

What does this mean for us?

God warns that he will punish all
who break these commandments.
Therefore we are to fear his wrath
and not disobey him.
But he promises grace and every
blessing to all who keep these
commandments.
Therefore we are to love and trust him,
and gladly do what he commands.

4

Sunday   *The First Commandment*

"I am the Lord . . ."

The dictionary tells us that a lord is a person who has power and authority, like a king. When we say that a person is powerful, we mean that he is strong, and when we say that he has authority, we mean that he gives commands. God is the greatest of all lords. God is king of heaven and earth. That is why he says, "I am *the* Lord." There is no one else who is as powerful or who has as much authority as God.

Here are some verses from a song (or psalm) that the Hebrews of the Old Testament times sang about the Lord and his power:

> Sing praises to God, sing praises!
>> Sing praises to our King, sing praises!
> For God is the king of all the earth;
>> Sing praises with a psalm!
> God reigns over the nations;
>> God sits on his holy throne.
>
> —Psalm 47:6-8

The following hymn is very much like the verses of the psalm we just read:

> *Rejoice, the Lord is King!*
>> *Your Lord and King adore;*
> *Rejoice, give thanks and sing,*
>> *And triumph evermore:*
> *Lift up your heart, lift up your voice;*
>> *Rejoice, again I say, rejoice.*
>
> *His kingdom cannot fail,*
>> *He rules o'er earth and heaven,*
> *The keys of death and hell*
>> *Are to our Jesus given:*
> *Lift up your heart, lift up your voice;*
>> *Rejoice, again I say, rejoice.*
>
> —436 SBH

PRAYER

Dear Lord, King of heaven and King of earth: I pray that you may be my King too. Help me always to obey your commands and be your faithful servant. Amen. The Lord's Prayer.

5

"I am ... your God."

Just what do we mean when we say "God"? Here again, the dictionary helps us. It says that God is someone who is more than human. If we think about this, we see that it must be true. God not only is the Lord of the heavens and the earth and of us, as we read yesterday, but he is the one who actually *made* the heavens and the earth, and he made us. Therefore he must certainly be more than we are—more than just human.

When we think of God, we think of someone whose wisdom is greater than any human wisdom, whose strength is greater than any human strength, and whose love is greater than any human love. And the wonderful thing about it is that this all-wise, all-powerful, all-loving God tells us that he is *our* God.

The 145th Psalm tells us what David, the famous king and psalm-writer of the Old Testament, thought about God:

> I will extol thee, my God and King,
>   and bless thy name for ever and ever.
> Every day I will bless thee,
>   and praise thy name for ever and ever.
> Great is the Lord, and greatly to be praised,
>   and his greatness is unsearchable.
>
> —Psalm 145:1-3

We tell God what we think of him in the following hymn:

My God, how wonderful thou art,
* Thy majesty how bright;*
How beautiful thy mercy-seat,
* In depths of burning light!*

Yet I may love thee, too, O Lord,
* Almighty as thou art,*
For thou hast stooped to ask of me
* The love of my poor heart.*

No earthly father loves like thee;
* No mother, e'er so mild,*
Bears and forbears as thou hast done
* With me, thy sinful child.*

—181 SBH

PRAYER

Dear God: I am thankful that you are greater than any human being, that you are strong enough to help me, and that you love me and want me to be yours. Amen. The Lord's Prayer.

"You shall have no other gods."

There is really only one *true* God, one more-than-human being whom we can worship and in whom we can put our trust. But people often worship things instead of God. These imitation gods or idols may be of stone or wood, like the Indians' totem poles; or we may worship money or fine clothes or success, making gods out of these things.

Whatever we put first in our lives, before anything else, is really our god. But worshiping false gods takes us away from the true God, who is the only one that can help us.

Even though the Hebrews, or Israelites, were God's people, they sometimes worshiped idols and had to be punished:

> And the Lord said to Moses, "Go down; for your people, whom you brought up out of the land of Egypt, have corrupted themselves; they have turned aside quickly out of the way which I commanded them; they have made for themselves a molten calf, and have worshiped it and sacrificed to it, and said, 'These are your gods, O Israel, who brought you up out of the land of Egypt!'" And the Lord said to Moses, "I have seen this people, and behold, it is a stiff-necked people; now therefore let me alone, that my wrath may burn hot against them and I may consume them . . ." —Exodus 32:7-10

In this hymn we confess that the same God who guided his people in olden times is our God too:

> *O God of Bethel, by whose hand*
> *Thy people still are fed;*
> *Who through this weary pilgrimage*
> *Hast all our fathers led:*
>
> *Such blessings from thy gracious hand*
> *Our humble prayers implore;*
> *And thou shalt be our chosen God,*
> *And portion evermore.*   —519 SBH

PRAYER

O one and only true God: Guide me in the right way so that I may never put false gods in your place. Help me to give all my worship and all my trust to you. Amen. The Lord's Prayer.

"We are to fear ... God above anything else."

We do not fear God enough these days. We say, "If God loves me, why should I be afraid of him?" Our parents love us, too, but we know they can punish us when we do wrong. This kind of fear is wholesome and keeps us in check. Those who disobey God are punished sooner or later. God is more powerful than any earthly parents, so we should fear his punishment most of all.

In the Book of Proverbs, or wise sayings, in the Old Testament, we find these verses about fearing God:

> The fear of the Lord is the beginning of knowledge.
> —Proverbs 1:7a

> The fear of the Lord is hatred of evil.
> —Proverbs 8:13a

> The fear of the Lord prolongs life.
> —Proverbs 10:27a

> The fear of the Lord is a fountain of life.
> —Proverbs 14:27a

We sing of the power and majesty of God in this hymn:

> *All hail the power of Jesus' Name!*
> *Let angels prostrate fall;*
> *Bring forth the royal diadem,*
> *And crown him Lord of all.*

> *Crown him, ye martyrs of your God*
> *Who from his altar call;*
> *Extol the Stem-of-Jesse's rod,*
> *And crown him Lord of all.*

> *Let every kindred, every tribe,*
> *On this terrestrial ball,*
> *To him all majesty ascribe,*
> *And crown him Lord of all.*
> —426 SBH, 339 LH

PRAYER

Dear God: When nothing else will keep me from doing what is wrong, help me to remember that those who disobey your commands are punished. May this thought bring me back again to you. Amen. The Lord's Prayer.

Thursday   *The First Commandment*

"We are to . . . love God above anything else."

Yesterday we said that sometimes it is only the fear of God that makes us obey him. But it pleases God most if we obey him because we love him, just as it pleases our parents much more if we do things for them because we love them rather than because we are afraid of being punished. No one else loves us as much as God does, and he hopes that our love for him will grow stronger day by day, so that we will love him more than anything or anyone else and so that obeying his commands will make us happy instead of unhappy. The more we love God, the easier it will be for us to do his will and to live a joyful life.

Before the people of Israel went into the land God had promised them for their home, Moses, the great leader who brought them through the wilderness, told them what God's commands for them were. One of the first things Moses said was:

> And you shall love the Lord your God with all your heart, and with all your soul, and with all your might.
> —Deuteronomy 6:5

This hymn tells God not only that we love him but also why we do:

> *How can I choose but love thee, God's dear Son,*
> *O Jesus, loveliest, and most loving One!*
> *Were there no heaven to gain, no hell to flee,*
> *For what thou art alone I must love thee.*
>
> *Not for the hope of glory or reward,*
> *But even as thyself hast loved me, Lord,*
> *I love thee, and will love thee and adore,*
> *Who art my King, my God, for evermore.*
> —489 SBH

PRAYER

Dear heavenly Father: May my love for you become stronger day by day so that I will not be happy unless I am doing your will. Amen. The Lord's Prayer.

"We are to . . . trust God above anything else."

We often hear people say about someone else, "I'd trust him with everything I have." That is the kind of trust or faith God wants us to have in him. He wants us to trust him with our lives, our souls, our futures. No matter how much trouble we may be in, no matter how much "bad luck" we may have, God wants us to trust him enough to believe that if we obey him, everything will turn out for our good. And if we do have such faith, we will find, as the years go by, that God does take care of us and that we can trust him, even though everyone else may fail us.

Some of the most beautiful words of trust in God that were ever spoken are in the Twenty-third Psalm:

> Even though I walk through the valley
> of the shadow of death,
> I fear no evil; for thou art with me;
> thy rod and thy staff, they comfort me.
>
> Psalm 23:4

Martin Luther wrote this great hymn of trust:

> *A mighty fortress is our God,*
> *A bulwark never failing;*
> *Our helper he amid the flood*
> *Of mortal ills prevailing:*
> *For still our ancient foe*
> *Doth seek to work us woe;*
> *His craft and power are great,*
> *And, armed with cruel hate,*
> *On earth is not his equal.*
>
> *Did we in our own strength confide*
> *Our striving would be losing;*
> *Were not the right Man on our side,*
> *The Man of God's own choosing.*
> *Dost ask who that may be?*
> *Christ Jesus, it is he;*
> *Lord Sabaoth his Name,*
> *From age to age the same,*
> *And he must win the battle.*
>
> —150 SBH, 262 LH

PRAYER

Dear Lord and Father: Help me to have faith like the psalmist's, that no matter what may happen, you will comfort and protect me. Amen. The Lord's Prayer.

Saturday   *The First Commandment*

" . . . above anything else."

Although our parents feed, clothe, and take care of us, we sometimes show them less love than we show our schoolmates. We may fear, love, and trust God, but we may fear or love or trust something or someone else even more. That is wrong. If we really believe that God is all-powerful, all-knowing, and all-loving, then we are foolish to fear, love, or trust anything or anyone else more than we do him. No other person or thing is as worthy of our love and trust as God. It is he who has made us, who makes it possible for us to stay alive, and who has saved us for his kingdom.

Abraham feared, loved, and trusted God above all things:

> By faith Abraham obeyed when he was called to go out to a place which he was to receive as an inheritance; and he went out, not knowing where he was to go. By faith he sojourned in the land of promise, as in a foreign land, living in tents with Isaac and Jacob, heirs with him of the same promise. For he looked forward to the city which has foundations, whose builder and maker is God.
> —Hebrews 11:8-10

This is one of the best-loved hymns of praise:

> *Praise to the Lord, the Almighty,*
> *the King of creation;*
> *O my soul, praise him, for he is thy*
> *health and salvation;*
> *All ye who hear,*
> *Now to his temple draw near;*
> *Joining in glad adoration.*
>
> *Praise to the Lord, O let all that*
> *is in me adore him;*
> *All that hath life and breath, come now*
> *with praises before him!*
> *Let the Amen*
> *Sound from his people again;*
> *Gladly for aye we adore him.*
> —408 SBH, 39 LH

PRAYER

Dear God: May I always fear, love, and trust you above all things. Amen. The Lord's Prayer.

11

"You shall not take the name of the Lord your God in vain."

Something that is vain is worthless or foolish. The name of God is certainly not worthless or foolish, but we can make it worthless if we use it for cheap things like swearing or jokes. That is like using a picture of your parents or best friend for a scratch pad. It was never intended to be used that way. We know how bad we feel when someone makes fun of our own name. The Lord's name is holy and should be used only for holy things like prayers and hymns. Otherwise, we use it in vain and we sin against God. We take God's name in vain when we use it disrespectfully and irreverently.

Instead of taking God's name in vain, we should treat it as a wonderful and holy name. There are many verses in the Psalms which praise the name of God:

Ascribe to the Lord the glory of his name;
worship the Lord in holy array.
—Psalm 29:2

Blessed be the name of the Lord from this time
forth and for evermore!
From the rising of the sun to its setting
the name of the Lord is to be praised!
—Psalm 113:2-3

We also praise the name of God in our hymns:

Thee we adore, eternal Lord!
We praise thy Name with one accord,
Thy saints, who here thy goodness see,
Through all the world do worship thee.

From day to day, O Lord, do we
Highly exalt and honor thee;
Thy Name we worship and adore,
World without end, for evermore!

—415 SBH

PRAYER

Dear Lord: May I never make foolish or worthless or disrespectful use of your name. Help me instead to honor and praise it and keep it holy. Amen. The Lord's Prayer.

Monday   *The Second Commandment*

"... so that we do not use his name to curse, swear ..."

When we curse or swear we really are asking for harm or injury to come to something or someone. A person may curse his car if it does not start on a cold winter morning, or curse his neighbor for making too much noise. When we use God's name to curse things, we cheapen his name, and that is a sin. But it is an even greater sin to use his name to curse people, because that is asking God to harm or even kill them. How awful it would be if some people's curses were really fulfilled!

If we use God's name to curse others, we may even harm ourselves. Read what God told Abraham, the father of the Jewish people:

> And I will make of you a great nation, and I will bless you, and make your name great, so that you will be a blessing. I will bless those who bless you, and him who curses you I will curse; and by you all the families of the earth will bless themselves.
>
> —Genesis 12:2-3

When we curse or swear, we are giving in to our tempers. In the following hymn we ask God to help us to be calm and peaceful:

> *Dear Lord and Father of mankind,*
>   *Forgive our foolish ways;*
> *Reclothe us in our rightful mind,*
> *In purer lives thy service find,*
>   *In deeper reverence praise.*
>
> *Drop thy still dews of quietness,*
>   *Till all our strivings cease;*
> *Take from our souls the strain and stress,*
> *And let our ordered lives confess*
>   *The beauty of thy peace.*
>
> *Breathe through the heats of our desire*
>   *Thy coolness and thy balm;*
> *Let sense be dumb, let flesh retire;*
> *Speak through the earthquake, wind, and fire,*
>   *O still small voice of calm!*
>
> —467 SBH

PRAYER

Dear heavenly Father: May I never use your name to hurt others, or wish them evil, but rather to bless and help them. Amen. The Lord's Prayer.

13

Tuesday   *The Second Commandment*

". . . so that we do not use his name to . . . lie, or deceive . . ."

Our God is a God of truth. The only real truth we have comes from him through his Word, which we call the Bible. But we hurt God if we use his name in telling lies or in any false dealings with others.

If we are to witness in court, for example, we are asked, "Do you promise to tell the truth, the whole truth, and nothing but the truth, so help you God?" If we answer that we do, but then say things that are *not* true, we have involved God's name in our lying, so that others think less of him. That is another vain, sinful way to use God's name.

In today's Bible reading the prophet Jeremiah talks with God about false prophets who use his name to tell the people lies:

> And the Lord said to me: "The prophets are prophesying lies in my name; I did not send them, nor did I command them or speak to them. . . . By sword and famine those prophets shall be consumed."
>
> —Jeremiah 14:14a and 15b

In the verses of the following hymn we call God the very spirit of truth. This is why it is so wrong to lie or deceive by his name:

> *Spirit of mercy, truth, and love,*
> *O shed thine influence from above,*
> *And still from age to age convey*
> *The wonders of this sacred day.*
>
> *Unfailing Comfort, heavenly Guide,*
> *Still o'er thy holy Church preside;*
> *Still let mankind thy blessings prove,*
> *Spirit of mercy, truth, and love.*
>
> —118 SBH

PRAYER

Dear God: May I never use your name to lie or be false, but rather to bring your word of truth to others. Amen. The Lord's Prayer.

Wednesday   *The Second Commandment*

"... but call on him ..."

Many people who believe that God made the world don't believe he is a God on whom they can call in a personal way. And yet this is exactly what Jesus was always trying to teach his followers to do. He told them to call God "Father" when they prayed to him. He told them that God had numbered all the hairs on their heads, and that not even the most common bird could be injured or killed without God's knowing about it.

"You are of more value than many sparrows," says Jesus. So, no matter how small or how large our problems are, our heavenly Father wants us to call on him because we are his children, and he loves us more than he loves any other part of his whole creation.

Many of the psalms are personal prayers, calling on God. These are some verses from such a psalm:

> Hear my prayer, O Lord;
>   let my cry come to thee!
> Do not hide thy face from me
>   in the day of my distress!
> Incline thy ear to me;
>   answer me speedily in the day
>   when I call!
>
> —Psalm 102:1-2

The following hymn tells how ready God is to help us if we call on him:

> *Come, ye disconsolate, where'er ye languish;*
> *Come to the mercy-seat, fervently kneel;*
> *Here bring your wounded hearts, here tell your anguish;*
> *Earth has no sorrow that heaven cannot heal.*
>
> *Joy of the desolate, light of the straying,*
> *Hope of the penitent, fadeless and pure!*
> *Here speaks the Comforter, tenderly saying,*
> *"Earth has no sorrow that heaven cannot cure."*
>
> —569 SBH, 531 LH

PRAYER

Dear heavenly Father: I thank you that you are ready to hear me whenever I call on you. May I always bring my problems and wants and needs to you, no matter how small or how big they are. Amen. The Lord's Prayer.

Thursday   *The Second Commandment*

" . . . but call on him in prayer . . ."

If we love God and need his help, we should want to talk with him often. We would never think of going for a week without talking to our parents or other members of the family, but some of us may go even longer than that without speaking to our heavenly Father.

Prayer is talking with God, or "calling on" him. Prayer is not some kind of ritual or service we go through to please God or to fulfill our spiritual duty, as some people think. Prayer is a very personal relationship between us and God, in which we tell him what is in our hearts and on our minds, thank and praise him, and ask for his guidance and help. We can talk to God at any time we feel a need to, but we should also set aside a definite time every day to call on God in prayer.

God's people have always been praying people. The Psalms are the great collection of the prayers of God's people.

> Give ear to my words, O Lord;
>   give heed to my groaning.
> Hearken to the sound of my cry,
>   my king and my God,
>   for to thee do I pray.
> O Lord, in the morning thou dost
>   hear my voice;
> in the morning I prepare a sacri-
>   fice for thee, and watch.
> —Psalm 5:1-3

This hymn tells of the importance of prayer:

> *Lord, teach us how to pray aright,*
> *With reverence and with fear;*
> *Though dust and ashes in thy sight,*
> *We may, we must draw near.*

> *God of all grace, we come to thee*
> *With broken, contrite hearts;*
> *Give what thine eye delights to see,*
> *Truth in the inward parts.*
> —452 SBH

PRAYER

Dear God: Help me to use the opportunity that prayer gives me to talk with you. May I have a regular time each day to pray. Amen. The Lord's Prayer.

16

Friday   *The Second Commandment*

"... but call on him in ... praise ..."

We praise people for things they have done: the soldier for his bravery, the scientist for a great discovery, the statesman for getting nations to agree on important matters, the fireman for saving a life. All these people are entitled to our praise because of what they have done.

And God should receive our praise and glory for what he has done! He has made us and the wonderful world around us; he protects us from danger; and he gave his only Son to save us from our sins. That is why we owe our greatest praise to him.

The word "praise" is used 153 times in the Psalms! In the 148th Psalm the writer pictures everything that God created as singing praises to him:

> Praise the Lord!
> Praise the Lord from the heavens,
>   praise him in the heights!
> Praise him, all his angels,
>   praise him, all his host!
>
> Praise him, sun and moon,
>   praise him, all you shining stars!
> —Psalm 148:1-3

There are many glorious hymns of praise which we sing in our church services. These are verses from one of the best known and best loved of our hymns of praise:

> *Praise to the Lord, the Almighty, the King of creation;*
> *O my soul, praise him, for he is thy health and salvation:*
>   *All ye who hear,*
>   *Now to his temple draw near;*
> *Joining in glad adoration.*
>
> *Praise to the Lord, who o'er all things so wondrously reigneth,*
> *Shelters thee under his wings, yea, so gently sustaineth:*
>   *Hast thou not seen?*
>   *All that is needful hath been*
> *Granted in what he ordaineth.*
>
> —408 SBH, 39 LH

PRAYER

Dear Lord: May I never forget to give you praise and glory for all the great and wonderful things you have done. Amen. The Lord's Prayer.

Saturday   *The Second Commandment*

". . . but call on him in . . . thanksgiving."

One of the things we most often forget is to be thankful. God has given us so many good things that we have forgotten to appreciate them. It is not enough to give praise to God for what he has done and let it go at that. We ought to feel continually thankful and grateful to him. Our thankfulness must also go deeper than for material things alone—for houses and clothes and food. We should be thankful for God's spiritual gifts to us as well.

The greatest gift that he has given us, the one for which we should be most thankful, is his dear Son, our Lord, who died on the cross to save us from our sins.

The 100th Psalm is a beautiful hymn of thanksgiving:

> Enter his gates with thanksgiving,
> and his courts with praise!
> Give thanks to him, bless his name!
> —Psalm 100:4

"Now Thank We All Our God" is one of the most famous of all the hymns we sing in the Lutheran Church.

> *Now thank we all our God*
> *With hearts and hands and voices,*
> *Who wondrous things hath done,*
> *In whom his world rejoices;*
> *Who, from our mother's arms,*
> *Hath blessed us on our way*
> *With countless gifts of love,*
> *And still is ours today.*
>
> *All praise and thanks to God*
> *The Father now be given,*
> *The Son, and him who reigns*
> *With them in highest heaven;*
> *The one eternal God,*
> *Whom earth and heaven adore;*
> *For thus it was, is now,*
> *And shall be evermore.*
> —443 SBH, 36 LH

PRAYER

Dear heavenly Father: May I never forget to be thankful for the many blessings you have given me. Amen. The Lord's Prayer.

Sunday   *The Third Commandment*

"Remember the Sabbath day, to keep it holy."

"Sabbath" comes from a Hebrew word meaning rest. The Sabbath day is a day of rest. God has commanded that we "remember" this day. When we work and are busy six days a week, we need one day of complete rest. That is the way God made us. Those who do not obey his command and seem to be too busy to rest on the Sabbath suffer in physical and mental health.

And God commanded us to keep the Sabbath "holy." Something is holy when it is set apart for God. We should set the Sabbath apart for him. We should attend services at church where we offer prayer, praise, and thanksgiving together with our fellow Christians. Attending church and Sunday school regularly is the surest way for us to obey God's command to "remember the Sabbath day, to keep it holy."

The words of the 95th Psalm are sung as a part of our Matins, or morning service, in the Lutheran Church. You will find them on page 131 of the *Service Book and Hymnal:*

> O come let us worship and bow down:
> let us kneel before the Lord our Maker.

This hymn tells of the blessings of worship on the Sabbath day:

> *To Thy temple I repair,*
> *Lord, I love to worship there,*
> *When, within the veil, I meet*
> *Christ before the mercy-seat.*
>
> *While Thy glorious praise is sung,*
> *Touch my lips, unloose my tongue,*
> *That my joyful soul may bless*
> *Thee, the Lord, my Righteousness.*
>
> *While Thy ministers proclaim*
> *Peace and pardon in Thy Name,*
> *Through their voice, by faith may I*
> *Hear Thee speaking from the sky.*
> —426 CSB, 2 LH

PRAYER

Dear heavenly Father: May I remember the Sabbath day and keep it holy by being in my place in God's house on Sunday morning. Amen. The Lord's Prayer.

Monday   *The Third Commandment*

"Six days you shall labor, and do all your work."

In the Bible, the above words form a part of the Third Commandment, "Remember the Sabbath day, to keep it holy."

God knows better than we do that as long as we are in the world we must go to school and later earn our living. He has given us six days out of seven for doing what the world demands of us, but he wants us to set aside the seventh day for him. That sounds fair enough, but, as you know, there are many people who do not set aside the Sabbath day for God. Six days are not enough to carry on their business; they need the seventh day also. Such people are too busy for their own good; they are too busy for God. When we do not take time out for God, we suffer. We must take care of our souls as well as our minds and bodies and business affairs.

Caesar was the ruler of the mighty Roman empire at the time Jesus lived. He stood for the world. Read what Jesus said about Caesar, or the world, and God:

> Jesus said to them, "Render to Caesar the things that are Caesar's, and to God the things that are God's."
> —Mark 12:17

Here is a hymn which tells us how our souls and hearts are helped by worshiping on the Sabbath:

> *Open now thy gates of beauty,*
>   *Zion, let me enter there,*
> *Where my soul in joyful duty,*
>   *Waits on him who answers prayer:*
> *O how blessed is this place,*
> *Filled with solace, light, and grace.*
>
> *Here, O God, I come before thee,*
>   *Come thou also down to me;*
> *Where we find thee and adore thee,*
>   *There a heaven on earth must be:*
> *To my heart O enter thou,*
> *Let it be thy temple now.*
>
> —187 SBH, 1 LH

PRAYER

Dear heavenly Father: Help me so to plan my work and play that I may be able to set aside one day out of the week for my soul. In Jesus' name. Amen. The Lord's Prayer.

Tuesday   *The Third Commandment*

"Therefore the Lord blessed the Sabbath day."

To bless means to make happy or prosperous. The Lord has made the Sabbath day a happy and prosperous one. He does not give us commandments just because he likes to see us obey them. He gives us commandments because he is our Father and knows what is best for us. If we set aside a day to worship and remember him and to rest from our regular work and study, we will receive God's blessing. We will be happier and more prosperous. The longer we live, the more we find out that we are always better off when we follow God's commands.

Instead of taking the attitude that a day set aside for God interferes with our work and spoils our week, we should believe that it gives us peace and strength to have a much better week.

From the beginning God made the Sabbath a day of rest.

> So God blessed the seventh day and hallowed it, because on it God rested from all his work which he had done in creation.   —Genesis 2:3

These verses are from another hymn about the Sabbath and tell us more reasons why it is the Lord's day:

> *O day of rest and gladness,*
>   *O day of joy and light,*
> *O balm of care and sadness,*
>   *Most beautiful, most bright!*
> *On thee the high and lowly,*
>   *Before the eternal throne,*
> *Sing, "Holy, holy, holy,"*
>   *To the great Three in One.*
>
> *On thee, at the creation,*
>   *The light first had its birth;*
> *On thee, for our salvation,*
>   *Christ rose from depths of earth;*
> *On thee our Lord victorious*
>   *The Spirit sent from heaven,*
> *And thus on thee most glorious*
>   *A triple light was given.*
>   —182 SBH, 9 LH

PRAYER

Dear heavenly Father: May I enjoy the blessing and prosperity of the Sabbath day all my life. In Jesus' name. Amen. The Lord's Prayer.

21

Wednesday   *The Third Commandment*

"We are to fear and love God so that we do not neglect his word."

Very few of us would say right out that we do not think very much of God's Word, the Bible, but we do not have to *say* it because our actions speak for us. If we let our Bibles stay on the bookshelf and never open them from week to week and month to month, we do not think very much of God's Word, no matter what we say. We are neglecting his Word, because we have it but do not read it. If we really do honor God's Word and know that we cannot live without it, then we will not neglect it.

The 119th Psalm is the longest psalm in the Bible. All 176 verses are in praise of God's Word:

> Oh, how I love thy law! It is my meditation all the day.
> Thy commandment makes me wiser than my enemies, for it
> is ever with me.
> I have more understanding than all my teachers, for thy
> testimonies are my meditation.
> I understand more than the aged, for I keep thy precepts.
> I hold back my feet from every evil way, in order to
> keep thy word.
> Thy word is a lamp to my feet and a light to my path.
> —Psalm 119:97-101 and 105

Another favorite among our hymns is this one about God's Word:

O Word of God incarnate,
O Wisdom from on high,
O Truth unchanged, unchanging,
O Light of our dark sky;
We praise thee for the radiance
That from the hallowed page,
A lantern to our footsteps,
Shines on from age to age.

The Church from her dear Master
Received the gift divine,
And still that light she lifteth
O'er all the earth to shine.
It is the golden casket
Where gems of truth are stored;
It is the heaven-drawn picture
Of Christ, the living Word.
—252 SBH, 294 LH

PRAYER

Dear heavenly Father: May I never neglect your Word; help me to read and hear it often so that I may learn to know and love it and so that it may be the guide of my life. In Jesus' name. Amen. The Lord's Prayer.

Thursday   *The Third Commandment*

"We are to fear and love God so that we do not neglect . . . the preaching of it."

There are very few young people who like to listen to sermons. In some cases, no doubt, the preacher has something to do with this, but most of the time it wouldn't make any difference who was doing the preaching. They would still rather not sit through a sermon.

It would help a great deal if they really understood what a sermon is. A sermon is an explanation of a certain part of the Word of God. That is, the preacher explains the Word from various angles so that it can be better understood, and he applies it to the problems of life. The sermon helps people to understand God's Word and to apply it to their lives. That is why people should not neglect preaching, but *want* to hear it.

The Word of God was first brought to people by preaching, long before it was put into any written form. That is still true today in some countries where missionaries work.

> But how are men to call upon him in whom they have not believed? And how are they to believe in him of whom they have never heard? And how are they to hear without a preacher?
> —Romans 10:14
> So faith comes from what is heard, and what is heard comes by the preaching of Christ.
> —Romans 10:17

In the words of the following hymn we ask God to bless our preachers:

> *Lord of the Church, we humbly pray*
> *For those who guide us in thy way,*
> *And speak thy holy word;*
> *With love divine their hearts inspire,*
> *And touch their lips with hallowed fire,*
> *And needful grace afford.*
> —303 SBH, 489 LH

PRAYER

Dear heavenly Father: Help me to make use of every opportunity to understand your Word better and also to tell it to others in my own way. In Jesus' name. Amen. The Lord's Prayer.

Friday   *The Third Commandment*

"We are to fear and love God so that we do not neglect his word . . . but regard it as holy."

One reason that we often do not pay more attention to God's Word is that we forget that it is God's Word. We see our Bible lying on the table and forget that it is not just another book by another author, but a holy Book. It comes from God himself. The Bible was written by men, it is true, but these men were chosen by God, and they wrote the words God inspired them to write. The Bible is still the best-selling book in the world. There is no other book like the Bible. It is the only word by which we are saved.

The first Psalm tells of the blessings that come to the person who studies the "Law" or Word of God.

> He is like a tree planted by streams of water,
> that yields its fruit in its season,
> and its leaf does not wither.
> In all that he does, he prospers.
>
> —Psalm 1:3

The following hymn tells how God's Word is holy because it shows us God himself. It is a favorite hymn of our church.

Shine Thou upon us, Lord,
True Light of men today,
And through the written Word
Thy very self display;
That so from hearts which burn
With gazing on Thy face,
Thy little ones may learn
The wonders of Thy grace.

Speak Thou for us, O Lord,
In all we say of Thee;
According to Thy Word
Let all our teaching be;
That so Thy lambs may know
Their own true Shepherd's voice
Where'er He leads them go,
And in His love rejoice.

—386 CSB

PRAYER

Dear heavenly Father: I thank you for my Bible. Help me to remember that it is a holy book because it comes from you. In Jesus' name. The Lord's Prayer.

Saturday   *The Third Commandment*

"We are to fear and love God so that we do not neglect his word ... but ... gladly hear and learn it."

Years ago most boys and girls learned their "three R's" in a one-room schoolhouse. Now young people take a great many more subjects and attend school in large buildings with dozens of rooms. A boy or girl in the eighth grade today knows much more about science and world affairs, for example, than eighth graders of fifty years ago knew. But how about the Bible? Do we know as much about God's Word as we know about other things? Do we spend as much time reading and studying God's Word as we do reading and studying other subjects? If we really believe that we cannot live our lives as God wants us to without understanding his Word, then we will gladly take the time to study it until it becomes a part of us.

St. Paul tells his young helper, Timothy, how important the Scriptures are for a person's life:

> But as for you, continue in what you have learned and have firmly believed, knowing from whom you learned it and how from childhood you have been acquainted with the sacred writings which are able to instruct you for salvation through faith in Christ Jesus. All scripture is inspired by God and profitable for teaching, for reproof, for correction, and for training in righteousness, that the man of God may be complete, equipped for every good work.
>
> —2 Timothy 3:14-17

People all over the world need God's Word to show them the right way of life. In this hymn we ask God to send his Word to every nation:

> *Spread, O spread, thou mighty word,*
> *Spread the kingdom of the Lord,*
> *That to earth's remotest bound*
> *Men may heed the joyful sound;*
>
> —323 SBH, 507 LH

PRAYER

Dear heavenly Father: Help me to take time out from my other studies to read and learn your Word. In Jesus' name. Amen. The Lord's Prayer.

Sunday   *The Fourth Commandment*

"Honor your father and your mother."

As young folks grow up, many of them begin to feel that it is no longer necessary to honor or respect their parents. There comes a time when they believe they are wiser than father and mother and no longer need their help or advice. Such an attitude is like saying that you can get along without food, after you have finished eating a big meal! If it were not for our parents' care and sacrifice and love, through sickness and trouble, many of us would not have lived to be as old as we are, and if parents did not give children a home and all that goes with it, life would be very dark indeed. Visit an orphans' home if you believe that having a father and mother makes no difference. That is why God commands us to honor parents; we owe everything to them.

St. Paul has advice for young people on how to treat their parents and also a word of advice for parents:

> Children, obey your parents in the Lord, for this is right. "Honor your father and mother" (this is the first commandment with a promise), "that it may be well with you and that you may live long on the earth." Fathers, do not provoke your children to anger, but bring them up in the discipline and instruction of the Lord.
>
> —Ephesians 6:1-4

In the following hymn we ask God to give us the love and obedience toward our parents that Jesus showed his mother and father:

> *O holy Lord, content to fill*
> *In lowly home the lowliest place,*
> *Thy childhood's law a mother's will,*
> *Obedience meek thy brightest grace;*
>
> *Lead every child that bears thy Name*
> *To walk in thine own guileless way,*
> *To dread the touch of sin and shame,*
> *And humbly, like thyself, obey.*
>
> —334 SBH

PRAYER

Dear heavenly Father: May I always be thankful for what my parents have done for me and honor them above everyone else. In Jesus' name. Amen. The Lord's Prayer.

26

"... that your days may be long in the land which the Lord your God gives you."

—Exodus 20:12

This statement in the Bible is usually taken to mean that any person who honors his parents will have a long life. That may or may not be so. The Ten Commandments were first given by God to the Hebrews as a *nation*. God was interested in them as separate persons, of course, but all together, they made up his Chosen People, or his nation. And so God is saying that the Hebrew nation will have a long life if the people honor their parents.

After thousands of years of persecution, the Hebrews have not been wiped out as a people; and in our own time they have come back to their "Promised Land" to establish a nation again. History teaches us that any nation in which family love and honor are strong (as has been true among the Jewish people) will outlive nations in which family life becomes weak and children no longer obey and honor their parents. May we in America learn this lesson well!

This verse says in a poetic way that the young person who does not honor his parents will suffer for it:

> The eye that mocks a father
> and scorns to obey a mother
> will be picked out by the ravens
> of the valley
> and eaten by the vultures.
>
> —Proverbs 30:17

This hymn is a prayer that God would guide us to live the way we ought:

> *O that the Lord would guide my ways*
> *To keep His statutes still!*
> *O that my God would grant me grace*
> *To know and do His will!*
>
> —275 CSB, 416 LH

PRAYER

Dear heavenly Father: Help me to appreciate all the blessings of my home and keep them by honoring Father and Mother. In Jesus' name. Amen. The Lord's Prayer.

The Fourth Commandment

"We are to fear and love God so that we do not despise ... our parents and others in authority ..."

We live in an age in which authority is not very popular. It is the fashion to think that each person is his own authority. A favorite American boast is, "I don't take orders from anybody."

Young people often feel that way about their parents, their teachers, their pastor. They despise or dislike anyone who tries to make them do anything, even if it is what they want to do! It is true that too much authority—dictatorship or tyranny—is bad. But it is also true that no authority, or mob rule, is even worse. For the sake of order we must have certain people who have authority, who give us orders, whom we obey. Nothing can be a success without a certain amount of order and discipline. It would be impossible to have homes, churches, schools, businesses, or governments if no one were in authority and everyone did just what he wanted to do.

The wise man who wrote the Book of Proverbs says:

> ... fools despise wisdom and instruction.
> Hear, my son, your father's instruction,
>   and reject not your mother's teaching.
> —Proverbs 1:7b and 8

In this hymn we ask that we may do God's will and practice love and obedience toward others:

> *May we Thy precepts, Lord, fulfil,*
> *And do on earth our Father's will,*
>   *As angels do above;*
> *Still walk in Christ, the living Way,*
> *With all Thy children, and obey*
>   *The law of Christian love.*
>
> *Spirit of life, of love and peace,*
> *Unite our hearts, our joy increase,*
>   *Thy gracious help supply;*
> *To each of us the blessing give,*
> *In Christian fellowship to live,*
>   *In joyful hope to die.*
>
> 269 CSB, 412 LH

PRAYER

Dear Lord: Help me willingly and cheerfully to obey and to respect those who teach and guide me. Amen. The Lord's Prayer.

Wednesday   *The Fourth Commandment*

"We are to fear and love God so that we do not . . . anger our parents and others in authority . . ."

When we disobey God, we not only hurt ourselves and others, but we hurt him, too. It makes God sad and disappointed that his children, whom he loves so much, should wilfully do what he does not want them to do and what is bad for them. Our parents and superiors feel the same way. They usually are trying to do what is best for us, and it often means sacrifice and hard work on their part. Nothing hurts your parents or your teachers or your pastor more than when you do something on purpose to displease them. It shows that you are not grateful for their efforts to give you a good home, a good education, to bring you to God. God never wants us to be ungrateful, but especially not to those who love and care for us.

How true are these words from the Book of Proverbs:

> A wise son makes a glad father,
>   but a foolish son is a sorrow to his mother.
> —Proverbs 10:1

In the following confirmation hymn, a young person pledges himself to be obedient to God's will, which would include the Fourth Commandment:

> *Lord, to thee I now surrender*
>   *All I have, and all I am;*
> *Make my heart more true and tender,*
>   *Glorify in me thy Name.*
>   *Let obedience, let obedience*
> *To thy will be all my aim.*
>
> *Help me in this high endeavor,*
>   *Father, Son, and Holy Ghost;*
> *Bind my heart to thee for ever*
>   *Till I join the heavenly host.*
>   *Living, dying, living, dying,*
> *Let me make in thee my boast.*
>
> —293 SBH

PRAYER

Dear heavenly Father: Help me to act and speak in such a way that I will not anger those who care and are trying to do their best for me. In Jesus' name. Amen. The Lord's Prayer.

Thursday   *The Fourth Commandment*

"... but ... obey ... them ..."

Every boy and girl who expects to grow up to be a useful, worthwhile man or woman must learn to obey, to do what he or she is told, to carry out orders. It is an old army saying that you can't be good at giving orders unless you are good at taking them. You can't be a real Christian without obeying, either. Jesus said that he came to do his Father's will—to obey his Father. And Jesus, in turn, gave his disciples, including all Christians, certain commands which he expects them to obey: to feed the hungry, clothe the naked, visit those in prison, be patient, be kind, be loving. We learn to obey by obeying our parents first of all. That is a part of honoring them, as God commands us to do. By obeying our parents we learn what is right and what is wrong, so that later on in life we will be able to make decisions for ourselves which will be right and pleasing to God.

The writer of the letter to the Hebrews, in the New Testament, says:

> Obey your leaders and submit to them; for they are keeping watch over your souls, as men who will have to give account. Let them do this joyfully, and not sadly, for that would be of no advantage to you.
> —Hebrews 13:17

This hymn reminds us that obedience is necessary because we are soldiers in the army of the Lord:

Onward, Christian soldiers,
Marching as to war,
With the Cross of Jesus
Going on before.
Christ the royal Master
Leads against the foe;
Forward into battle,
See, his banners go!

Like a mighty army
Moves the Church of God;
Brothers, we are treading
Where the saints have trod.
We are not divided,
All one body we,
One in hope and doctrine,
One in charity.
—560 SBH, 658 LH

PRAYER

Dear heavenly Father: Help me to be obedient to my earthly superiors so that I will be obedient to you. Amen. The Lord's Prayer.

Friday   *The Fourth Commandment*

". . . but . . . love . . . them"

Jesus tells us that if we love one another, we automatically carry out all God's other commandments. It works the same way with our parents and others in authority. If we love them, we will want to honor them. If we love our parents, we will want to obey them rather than displease them. If we have no love in us, our honor and our service and our obedience will not be very pleasing either to God or to our parents and superiors. If we do these things because we have to rather than because we want to, we cannot be very happy; but if we do them out of love, God will bless us with a useful, happy life.

> Love is patient and kind; love is not jealous or boastful; it is not arrogant or rude. Love does not insist on its own way; it is not irritable or resentful; it does not rejoice at wrong, but rejoices in the right.   —1 Corinthians 13:4-6

In the following hymn we ask God for his love in our hearts, so that we can love others. "Alpha and Omega" are the first and last letters of the Greek alphabet and stand for Jesus as being the beginning and the end of our lives.

> *Love divine, all loves excelling,*
> *Joy of heaven, to earth come down!*
> *Fix in us thy humble dwelling,*
> *All thy faithful mercies crown.*
> *Jesus, thou art all compassion,*
> *Pure unbounded love thou art;*
> *Visit us with thy salvation,*
> *Enter every trembling heart.*
>
> *Breathe, O breathe thy loving spirit*
> *Into every troubled breast;*
> *Let us all in thee inherit,*
> *Let us find thy promised rest.*
> *Take away the love of sinning;*
> *Alpha and Omega be;*
> *End of faith, as its beginning,*
> *Set our hearts at liberty.*
>   —397 SBH, 351 LH

PRAYER

Dear heavenly Father: Help me to follow the example of Jesus and obey, love, and serve my parents and others in authority because I love them. In Jesus' name. Amen. The Lord's Prayer.

Saturday   *The Fourth Commandment*

". . . and serve them."

The words "serve" and "servant" are used not only in connection with hired servants like maids and butlers. To serve also means to do one's duty. Soldiers serve in the army, and a person is called to serve on a jury or church council. We speak of our congressmen and even our presidents as public servants. When we serve our parents and those in authority, we are doing only our God-given duty. The home cannot go on very well unless all members of the family do their duty, unless each one serves as best he can. School or church or government could not exist if people did not serve or do their duty towards their fellow man. The idea of service, just like the idea of authority, is not very popular today. Almost everyone, including young people at home, want high pay before they will do what ought to be their simple duty. But service is as important to the home and society as authority. Our civilization depends on service, on doing our duty to God and man.

Jesus, who gave us our greatest example of loving service, has this to say about it:

> But whoever would be great among you must be your servant, and whoever would be first among you must be your slave; even as the Son of man came not to be served but to serve, and to give his life as a ransom for many.
> —Matthew 20:26b-28

Here we ask Jesus to help us follow his example of service to others:

> *O Master, let me walk with thee*
> *In lowly paths of service free;*
> *Tell me thy secret; help me bear*
> *The strain of toil, the fret of care.*
>
> *Teach me thy patience; still with thee*
> *In closer, dearer company,*
> *In work that keeps faith sweet and strong,*
> *In trust that triumphs over wrong.*
> —537 SBH

PRAYER

Dear heavenly Father: Make me a cheerful servant. Help me to do my duty to my parents and to those in authority and especially to you. In Jesus' name. Amen. The Lord's Prayer.

Sunday   *The Fifth Commandment*

"You shall not kill."

To kill means to take life. The world is full of life that God created, from the tiniest one-celled creatures that we need a microscope to see, to the highest of all God's creatures, man himself. Everything that has life gets that life from God. We cannot give life to anything. Therefore, since we cannot create life, we certainly do not have the right to destroy it. We should think twice before we kill any living thing. We should always ask ourselves the question: "Is it necessary, or for a good cause?" If we think of all living things as created by God for man's necessary use and enjoyment, we will not kill just to take life. The great missionary, Albert Schweitzer, encourages people to have reverence for life because all life comes from God.

Jesus loved the world of nature that his Father had created. He spoke very often of the beauty of living things:

> Look at the birds of the air: they neither sow nor reap nor gather into barns, and yet your heavenly Father feeds them. Are you not of more value than they?
> —Matthew 6:26

> And why are you anxious about clothing? Consider the lilies of the field, how they grow; they neither toil nor spin; yet I tell you, even Solomon in all his glory was not arrayed like one of these.
> —Matthew 6:28-29

In this well-loved hymn we thank God for his created world:

> *For the beauty of the earth,*
> *For the beauty of the skies,*
> *For the love which from our birth*
> *Over and around us lies,*
> *Christ, our God, to thee we raise*
> *This our sacrifice of praise.*
>
> *For the beauty of each hour*
> *Of the day and of the night,*
> *Hill and vale, and tree and flower,*
> *Sun and moon and stars of light,*
> *Christ, our God, to thee we raise*
> *This our sacrifice of praise.*
> —444 SBH

PRAYER

Dear heavenly Father: I thank you for the beauty of life that is all around me. Help me to love and protect it. In Jesus' name. Amen. The Lord's Prayer.

33

"You shall not kill."

We have said that human life is God's highest creation. When one person takes the life of another person, that is murder. The Bible tells us that God created man in his own image. The Bible also tells us that our bodies are the temples of God and that our souls belong to God. In other words, when we take human life we take what is God's—what God created for himself. That is why murder is one of the most awful sins. We do not actually have to kill someone with our own hands to be guilty before God. St. John said that he who hates his brother is a murderer. We often hear the expression, "If looks could kill, he'd be dead." That is exactly what Jesus meant. If we would like to injure someone, but hold back because we know we would get into trouble, God considers us just as guilty as though we had gone through with it. It is what is in our hearts that counts with God.

Here are the actual words of Jesus about killing and hatred:

> "You have heard that it was said to the men of old, 'You shall not kill; and whoever kills shall be liable to judgment.' But I say to you that every one who is angry with his brother shall be liable to judgment; whoever insults his brother shall be liable to the council, and whoever says 'You fool!' shall be liable to the hell of fire."
>
> —Matthew 5:21-22

The words of this hymn ask God for strength to live in love with our fellow men:

> *Shepherd of souls, refresh and bless*
> *Thy chosen pilgrim flock*
> *With manna in the wilderness,*
> *With water from the rock.*
>
> *Be known to us in breaking bread,*
> *But do not then depart;*
> *Saviour, abide with us, and spread*
> *Thy table in our heart.*
>
> —269 SBH

PRAYER

Dear heavenly Father: Take away all thoughts and feelings that would hurt others. May I never end the day being angry with anyone. In Jesus' name. Amen. The Lord's Prayer.

Tuesday   *The Fifth Commandment*

"We are to fear and love God so that we do not hurt our neighbor in any way."

The newspapers often carry stories about people who purposely harm or even kill others. More and more, the ones guilty of such terrible crimes are young people in their teens who roam the city streets in groups, actually looking for someone to hurt. Such people have no fear of God and certainly do not think of their fellow human beings as God's greatest, most precious creation. We have been created in God's image or likeness. Therefore, when we harm one another, we sin against God.

If we really love God, we will not be able to hurt others. St. John says:

> If anyone says, "I love God," and hates his brother, he is a liar; for he who does not love his brother whom he has seen, cannot love God whom he has not seen. And this commandment we have from him, that he who loves God should love his brother also.
>
> —1 John 4:20-21

We ask in this hymn that we may follow Christ's example toward others:

> *Teach us the lesson thou hast taught,*
> *To feel for those thy Blood hath bought,*
> *That every word and deed and thought*
> *May work a work for thee.*

> *For all are brethren, far and wide,*
> *Since thou, O Lord, for all hast died;*
> *Then teach us, whatsoe'er betide,*
> *To love them all in thee.*
>
> —316 SBH, 439 LH

PRAYER

Dear heavenly Father: Keep me from doing or saying anything that could lead to the injury of someone else; and help me always to do what I can to stop others from being hurt. In Jesus' name. Amen. The Lord's Prayer.

"... but help him ..."

There are many ways we can help others if we will only look for them. Think of all the help you can give at home. You could make it easier for Mother to take more time off from her never-ending work if you would offer to do the dishes or vacuum the rug on Saturday. Dad needs help with the storm windows or cleaning the cellar or mowing the lawn. If you have younger brothers or sisters, they might need help with their homework, or they may want you to fix their tricycle or dolls. Your school buddy might need you to take his paper route for a couple of days or to help him set up a dark room to develop pictures. God wants us to help one another. No person can live for one day without some kind of help from someone. And the more we help, the better life will be for us as well as for those we help.

Jesus' story of the Good Samaritan tells how some people did their neighbor bodily harm and injury but another person helped him:

> But a Samaritan, as he journeyed, came to where he was; and when he saw him, he had compassion, and went to him and bound up his wounds, pouring on oil and wine; then he set him on his own beast and brought him to an inn, and took care of him.
>
> —Luke 10:33-34

We ask in this hymn to be able to follow in Jesus' steps and do good to others:

> *O brother man, fold to thy heart thy brother!*
> *Where pity dwells, the peace of God is there;*
> *To worship rightly is to love each other,*
> *Each smile a hymn, each kindly deed a prayer.*
>
> *Follow with reverent steps the great example*
> *Of him whose holy work was doing good;*
> *So shall the wide earth seem our Father's temple,*
> *Each loving life a psalm of gratitude.*
>
> —539 SBH

PRAYER

Dear heavenly Father: May I follow the example of Jesus and be helpful wherever I am needed. In Jesus' name. Amen. The Lord's Prayer.

Thursday   *The Fifth Commandment*

"... but help him ..."

One way to help others is to comfort them. To comfort means to give cheer, hope, and strength. How many people in this old world of ours need cheer, hope, and strength! We somehow think that Mother and Dad are made of iron and can go on forever without needing any comfort. But if we made it our business to watch, we would see that there are often times when our parents could use a little cheering up from us. Sick people need our comfort most of all. If there is anyone you know who has been ill for more than a week, pay him a visit and bring something or say something that will give cheer and hope. Don't forget to say a prayer for him. Or if you know someone who is old and who has had to stay indoors for a long time, that person would get comfort from your visit. If you have a pal who has the "blues," he needs your cheer. The early Christians got to be known because they loved and helped one another. That is the way Christians will always be known.

Jesus often spoke words of peace and comfort to his disciples and he speaks them to us also:

> Peace I leave with you; my peace I give to you; not as the world gives do I give to you. Let not your hearts be troubled, neither let them be afraid.
>
> —John 14:27

Here is a hymn that says it is a privilege to bring comfort to others:

> *O hearts are bruised and dead,*
> *And homes are bare and cold,*
> *And lambs for whom the Shepherd bled*
> *Are straying from the fold;*
>
> *To comfort and to bless,*
> *To find a balm for woe,*
> *To tend the lone and fatherless,*
> *Is angels' work below.*
>
> —544 SBH, 441 LH

PRAYER

Dear heavenly Father: May I follow the example of Jesus and comfort those whom I know need hope and cheer. In Jesus' name. Amen. The Lord's Prayer.

Friday   *The Fifth Commandment*

"... but help him in all his physical needs."

All of us know about the "fair weather" kind of friend—the one who is always around when things are going well with us, but who somehow always disappears just when we need a friend the most. There is an old saying that "a friend in need is a friend indeed." If we want to be real friends to others, we will see to it that we are there to assist and comfort them when they are in danger or trouble. It might mean helping an old person or a little child who is trying to get across a street full of traffic; it might mean staying with your pal who just hit a ball through a window and admitting you were on the team too; it might mean calling an ambulance or a doctor if your friend is suddenly hurt or taken ill. Jesus gave his life for us who are in danger because of sin. If we are his disciples, we will follow his example and help others who are in danger and trouble.

Jesus performed miracles to show that he was really the Lord of all life and that we can come to him for comfort in any kind of danger or want. That is why he calmed the storm for his disciples on the Sea of Galilee:

> And a great storm of wind arose, and the waves beat into the boat, so that the boat was already filling. But he was in the stern, asleep on the cushion; and they woke him and said to him, "Teacher, do you not care if we perish?" And he awoke and rebuked the wind, and said to the sea, "Peace! Be still!" And the wind ceased, and there was a great calm.
> —Mark 4:37-39

This hymn, based on our Bible passage for today, asks Jesus to help us through all of life's dangers:

> *Jesus, Saviour, pilot me*
> *Over life's tempestuous sea;*
> *Unknown waves before me roll,*
> *Hiding rock and treacherous shoal;*
> *Chart and compass come from thee,*
> *Jesus, Saviour, pilot me.*
>
> —531 SBH, 649 LH

PRAYER

Dear heavenly Father: May I follow the example of Jesus and be ready to help those who are in danger and trouble. In Jesus' name. Amen. The Lord's Prayer.

"... but help him in all his physical needs."

There always have been and probably always will be poor people in the world. We could say about the poor people what Abraham Lincoln said about the common people: that God must love them because he made so many of them. Perhaps God wants to see if we are going to do anything to help them. Perhaps some day when we stand before God's throne one of the first things he will ask us is what we did to help those in want—the poor. In even the best schools there are some young people who come from poor homes where there is barely enough food to eat or clothes to wear. Do you have such a classmate? Have you tried to help him or asked your parents to find out about his family and what they need? Have you given any of your own money or clothes to Lutheran Welfare or Lutheran World Action to bring assistance and comfort to those in your state and in foreign lands who are in want? All these are ways in which we can follow Jesus' example of helping the poor.

In the following passage Jesus tells us that whatever we do for others who are in need, we do for him:

> And the King will answer them, "Truly, I say to you, as you did it to one of the least of these my brethren, you did it to me."
>
> —Matthew 25:40

When we sing this hymn, we ask for inspiration to help others in want:

> *In haunts of wretchedness and need,*
> *On shadowed thresholds dark with fears,*
> *From paths where hide the lures of greed,*
> *We catch the vision of thy tears.*
>
> *The cup of water given for thee*
> *Still holds the freshness of thy grace;*
> *Yet long these multitudes to see*
> *The sweet compassion of thy face.*
>
> —351 SBH

PRAYER

Dear heavenly Father: Open my heart to the needs of others and help me to share what I have with them. In Jesus' name. Amen. The Lord's Prayer.

"You shall not commit adultery."

To adulterate means to spoil something which is pure and clean by adding something to it which does not belong. For example, manufacturers used to adulterate breakfast foods by adding sawdust to them! To stop such cheating, Congress passed a law known as the National Food and Drug Act. The people of our country wanted pure, *unadulterated* foods. Well, human beings, whom God made to be pure and clean, can become adulterated, too, and can be spoiled by things which do not belong. Our minds can become adulterated by unclean thoughts, and our bodies can become adulterated by unclean actions. That is why God gives us the Sixth Commandment—a Pure Thought and Action Law—so that our minds and bodies may be clean and pure as he intended them to be.

In his Letter to the Ephesians, St. Paul warns them that God will punish those who live impure lives:

> But immorality and all impurity or covetousness must not even be named among you, as is fitting among saints. . . . Be sure of this, that no immoral or impure man, or one who is covetous (that is, an idolator), has any inheritance in the kingdom of Christ and of God. Let no one deceive you with empty words, for it is because of these things that the wrath of God comes upon the sons of disobedience.
>
> -Ephesians 5:3, 5 and 6

We ask God in the following hymn to make us pure like Jesus:

> *O for a heart to praise my God,*
> *A heart from sin set free!*
> *A heart that always feels thy Blood*
> *So freely shed for me;*
>
> *A humble, lowly, contrite heart,*
> *Believing, true, and clean,*
> *Which neither life nor death can part*
> *From him that dwells within.*
>
> —389 SBH

PRAYER

Dear Lord Jesus: Help me to be clean in what I think and say and do, so that I may be your servant. Amen. The Lord's Prayer.

Monday   *The Sixth Commandment*

"... in matters of sex ... pure and honorable": in thought.

Even though the word "thoughts" is not included in the explanation to the Sixth Commandment, God does want us to be pure and honorable in our thoughts about sex as well as in our words and deeds. What we say and do usually depends on what we have first thought. The dictionary tells us that the word "sex" means all the things that have to do with a boy's or man's being different from a girl or woman. In the marriage ceremony of our church we repeat Jesus' words that God made people male and female, or men and women, in order that they could become husbands and wives and fathers and mothers. This is what we are actually talking about when we use the word "sex." It is a wonderful miracle of God, and rather than having any nasty or impure thoughts about it, we should be happy and thankful that he has made us as we are.

St. Paul tells us to form the habit of thinking good thoughts:

> Finally, brethren, whatever is true, whatever is honorable, whatever is just, whatever is pure, whatever is lovely, whatever is gracious, if there is any excellence, if there is anything worthy of praise, think about these things.
>
> —Philippians 4:8

This hymn says that Jesus can give us pure minds:

> *Thou art the Truth; thy word alone*
> *True wisdom can impart;*
> *Thou only canst inform the mind*
> *And purify the heart.*

> *Thou art the Way, the Truth, the Life;*
> *Grant us that way to know,*
> *That truth to keep, that life to win,*
> *Whose joys eternal flow.*
>
> —390 SBH, 355 LH

PRAYER

Dear Lord Jesus: Help me to keep my mind pure so that I can use it to serve you. Amen. The Lord's Prayer.

". . . so that in matters of sex our words . . . are pure and honorable . . ."

The first thing that many soldiers wanted when they returned from overseas in the last war was a telephone booth where they could talk to their loved ones again. It is by words that we express our love; it is by words that we teach others; it is by words that we carry on our business; it is by words that we worship God. All these uses of words come under the heading of "communication." God gave us speech so that we could communicate with one another and with him. Speech can be spoiled or adulterated, just as our thoughts can. Lying, cursing, telling dirty jokes about sex—these are things which God never intended to be part of our speech. These spoil our speech and let the devil make use of it. Before we know it, filthy speech becomes a habit very hard to break. Instead of being a means of communication, our speech becomes the devil's tool to make us ashamed of our bodies.

As Christians we should always think of what effect our words have on others and how they reflect on us and our Lord. Jesus said:

". . . not what goes into the mouth defiles a man, but what comes out of the mouth, this defiles a man."
—Matthew 15:11

We pray God in this hymn that we may use our voices in a pure and honorable way to benefit others:

Lord, speak to me, that I may speak
In living echoes of thy tone;
As thou hast sought, so let me seek
Thy erring children lost and lone.

O teach me, Lord, that I may teach
The precious things thou dost impart;
And wing my words, that they may reach
The hidden depths of many a heart.

—538 SBH

PRAYER

Dear Lord Jesus: Help me to keep my speech pure so that I can use it to serve you. Amen. The Lord's Prayer.

". . . so that in matters of sex . . . our conduct [is] pure and honorable . . ."

To be a Christian means to be a follower of Christ. To follow Christ means to try to follow his example—and he lived a pure and perfect life. No one can honestly call himself a Christian, or a follower of Christ, if he leads an unclean life. The two just don't go together. St. Paul tells us that our bodies are the temples of God. If that is true, we sin against him when we sin against our bodies or any other person's body. There is a certain age when questions come into the minds of most young people about their own bodies and the bodies of others. That is the time to remember that our bodies were given to us by God— not to treat like playthings and to use in secret, shameful ways, but to keep clean and strong and honorable in order that they may serve us through a long and useful life to his glory and in the service of others.

The Apostle Paul had this advice and a warning about our bodies:

> Do you not know that you are God's temple and that God's Spirit dwells in you? If any one destroys God's temple, God will destroy him. For God's temple is holy, and that temple you are.
>
> —1 Corinthians 3:16-17

The following hymn asks God to make us his temple.

> *Blest are the pure in heart,*
> *For they shall see their God,*
> *The secret of the Lord is theirs,*
> *Their soul is Christ's abode.*
>
> *Lord, we thy presence seek,*
> *Ours may this blessing be;*
> *Give us a pure and lowly heart,*
> *A temple meet for thee.*
>
> —394 SBH

PRAYER

Lord Jesus: Help me to keep my actions pure so that I may serve you in whatever I do. Amen. The Lord's Prayer.

43

Thursday   *The Sixth Commandment*

". . . and husband and wife love and respect each other."

These days too many husbands and wives fail to obey God's Word. There is not enough love and honor between many husbands and wives. That is why one of every three homes breaks up in our country. Whenever God's commands are not obeyed, the results are bad. Young people must begin early to show love and honor toward their parents and toward each other so that when the time comes for them to marry, they will have formed the right habits for living together as Christians.

The following advice of the Apostle Paul is a part of the marriage ceremony of our Lutheran Church:

> Wives, be subject to your husbands, as to the Lord. Husbands, love your wives, as Christ loved the church and gave himself up for her.
>
> —Ephesians 5:22 and 25

This hymn is sung at many church weddings, and we should take its words to heart:

> *O perfect Love, all human thought transcending,*
> *Lowly we kneel in prayer before thy throne,*
> *That theirs may be the love which knows no ending,*
> *Whom thou for evermore dost join in one.*

> *Grant them the joy which brightens earthly sorrow;*
> *Grant them the peace which calms all earthly strife,*
> *And to life's day the glorious unknown morrow*
> *That dawns upon eternal love and life.*
>
> —300 SBH, 623 LH

PRAYER

Dear Lord Jesus: Help us to love and honor each other so that our homes will receive your blessing. Amen. The Lord's Prayer.

44

Friday   *The Sixth Commandment*

". . . and husband and wife love . . . each other."

When a man and a woman are married in the Lutheran Church, each one promises to love, comfort, honor and keep the other in sickness and in health, as well as to "forsake" all other people, if necessary, and keep only to each other so long as they both shall live. That is a serious promise to make, and an impossible one to keep without God's help. Only people who are used to doing God's will and who want his will to be done in their lives can keep such a promise. Human love alone can not keep us together through all the ups and downs of life, but God's love goes from our hearts to other people and keeps us faithful and true.

St. John tells us that real love comes only from God:

> In this the love of God was made manifest among us, that God sent his only Son into the world, so that we might live through him. In this is love, not that we loved God but that he loved us and sent his Son to be the expiation for our sins. Beloved, if God so loved us, we also ought to love one another.
>
> —1 John 4:9-11

The following hymn asks God's blessing on those who are married in the church:

> *On those who at thine altar kneel,*
> *O Lord, thy blessing pour,*
> *That each may wake the other's zeal*
> *To love thee more and more;*
>
> *O grant them here in peace to live,*
> *In purity and love,*
> *And, this world leaving, to receive*
> *A crown of life above.*
>
> —301 SBH, 620 LH

PRAYER

Dear Lord Jesus: Help me to love others with the same love you have shown me. Amen. The Lord's Prayer.

Saturday   *The Sixth Commandment*

". . . and husband and wife . . . respect each other."

Just as love for one's husband or wife depends on the kind of life a person lives before marriage, so respect depends on it too. If we have been in the habit of thinking low and filthy thoughts about ourselves and others, especially about our bodies, how will we be able to honor and respect each other after marriage? The same holds true of impure actions. If we have used our bodies in shameful ways, and not treated them as God's temples, how will we be able to honor our bodies after marriage? We are like a building: we are no better than our foundations. And we build our foundations when we are young. If we respect others in our youth, we will do so the rest of our lives.

Jesus says we should build our lives on the foundation of God's Word:

> Every one who comes to me and hears my words and does them, I will show you what he is like: he is like a man building a house, who dug deep, and laid the foundation upon rock; and when a flood arose, the stream broke against that house, and could not shake it, because it had been well built.
> —Luke 6:47-48

In the words of this hymn we ask Jesus to help us build good foundations for life:

O Jesus, I have promised
  To serve thee to the end;
Be thou for ever near me,
  My master and my friend;
I shall not fear the battle
  If thou art by my side,
Nor wander from the pathway
  If thou wilt be my guide.

O let me hear thee speaking
  In accents clear and still,
Above the storms of passion,
  The murmurs of self-will;
O speak to reassure me,
  To hasten or control;
O speak, and make me listen,
  Thou guardian of my soul.
—515 SBH

PRAYER

Dear heavenly Father: Help me to prepare for the respect that marriage needs by living a pure life now. Amen. The Lord's Prayer.

Sunday   *The Seventh Commandment*

"You shall not steal."

So often we think of God's commandments and the rules our parents lay down for us as disagreeable things that take the joy out of life. We hardly ever stop to figure out why those commandments and rules were made. If we did, we would find that they really make it possible to keep the joy in life.

For example, let us suppose that God had never given us the Seventh Commandment and that stealing was not considered wrong. That would mean that no one would be able to call anything his own because anyone else could take it away from him at any time—his car, his clothes, his money, his food, his family. There would be no policemen to stop stealing, and no laws against it. What an awful world this would be! The joy would certainly be taken out of life! God *does* have a reason for giving us the Ten Commandments. He created us, and he knows what rules are best for us to live by in order to lead happy, useful lives.

St. Paul told people that when they become Christians, they must give up stealing:

> Let the thief no longer steal, but rather let him labor, doing honest work with his hands, so that he may be able to give to those in need.
> —Ephesians 4:28

This hymn praises the wisdom of God's Word:

O Word of God incarnate
O Wisdom from on high,
O Truth unchanged, unchang-
ing,
O Light of our dark sky;
We praise thee for the radiance
That from the hallowed page,
A lantern to our footsteps,
Shines on from age to age.

It floateth like a banner
Before God's host unfurled;
It shineth like a beacon
Above the darkling world;
It is the chart and compass
That o'er life's surging sea,
'Mid mists and rocks and quick-
sands,
Still guides, O Christ to thee.
—252 SBH, 294 LH

PRAYER

Dear heavenly Father: Help me to understand that your commandments are for our own protection and happiness. In Jesus' name. Amen. The Lord's Prayer.

47

Monday   *The Seventh Commandment*

"We are to fear and love God so that we do not take our neighbor's money."

Money has value because of what it stands for. If a man has a hundred dollars in his account at the bank, it may mean that he has given a hundred dollars' worth of service to someone or that he has sold someone a hundred dollars' worth of goods. Money stands for goods and services. When you take a person's money from him, you have made him work for nothing or given away his goods for nothing. You have also stopped him from using his money to buy other goods and services he needs and wants. So, when we steal money, we really sin twice against the person from whom we steal. We also sin in another way. If we spend the money, then we are getting goods and services which we have not earned and do not deserve.

All these are reasons why God commands us not to steal money. The Bible warns us about letting a desire for money tempt us to do wrong:

> But those who desire to be rich fall into temptation, into a snare, into many senseless and hurtful desires that plunge men into ruin and destruction. For the love of money is the root of all evils; it is through this craving that some have wandered away from the faith and pierced their hearts with many pangs.
>
> —1 Timothy 6:9-10

In this hymn we ask for a pure heart free from temptation:

> O for a heart to praise my God,
>   A heart from sin set free!
> A heart that always feels thy Blood
>   So freely shed for me;
>
> A heart in every thought renewed
>   And full of love divine;
> Perfect, and right, and pure, and good,
>   A copy, Lord, of thine.
>
> —389 SBH

PRAYER

Dear heavenly Father: Help me never to do what is wrong because of money. May I love your commandments more than money. In Jesus' name. Amen. The Lord's Prayer.

The Seventh Commandment

"... so that we do not take our neighbor's money ..."

We know that if we take money out of our schoolmate's jacket which is hanging in the cloakroom, that is stealing. But there is another way of stealing money that is not as open but much more common: that is, charging too much for goods or services that we give. We are living in times when all of us are being robbed by high prices. Hardly anything we buy is worth the price we must pay for it these days. If you take a job baby-sitting or washing windows or shoveling snow, and you charge as much as you think you can get instead of trying to figure out what a fair price would be, you are stealing other people's money just as surely as if you took it from their pocketbook. Using the excuse that "everyone else does it" can't make it right.

God wants us to serve and help others rather than rob them. More than a thousand years before Christ, God told his people:

> You shall not oppress your neighbor or rob him. The wages of a hired servant shall not remain with you all night until the morning.
> —Leviticus 19:13

This hymn asks for strength to overcome our desires to sin against others:

> *May earthly feelings die,*
> *And fruits of faith increase;*
> *And Adam's nature prostrate lie*
> *Before the Prince of Peace.*

> *Endue us, Lord, with strength*
> *To triumph over sin:*
> *That we may with Thy saints at length*
> *Eternal glory win.*
> —265 CSB

PRAYER

Dear heavenly Father: Help me never to steal money from others by charging more than my services are worth. In Jesus' name. Amen. The Lord's Prayer.

"... so that we do not take our neighbor's money ..."

There is still another way by which we rob our neighbor of his money: by not giving a full hour's work for a full hour's pay. We hear a lot nowadays about higher wages and shorter hours. We seldom hear anything about doing better work or working harder. The quality of workmanship has gone down everywhere until now it is a rare thing to find some little shop that still puts out high quality work for a decent price. Most people today work to get money and are not interested in how they do their job, nor do they care how much they loaf on the job.

When we do not give our best for our pay, we are stealing our employer's money. If you are being paid 60c an hour to wash storm windows and wash only five windows in an hour when you could wash seven or eight, you are stealing about 20c an hour from the person who hired you. Or if you don't get the windows clean, but leave them full of smears, you are stealing money, too. When you get paid for services you do not actually perform, you are breaking the Seventh Commandment.

St. Paul describes the proper attitude a Christian ought to have when he works:

> ... rendering service with a good will as to the Lord and not to men, knowing that whatever good any one does, he will receive the same again from the Lord, whether he is a slave or free.
>
> —Ephesians 6:7-8

Here is a hymn in which we ask God to keep us obedient to his Word:

Let me be thine forever,
  My gracious God and Lord;
May I forsake thee never,
  Nor wander from thy word.
Preserve me from the mazes
  Of error and distrust,
And I shall sing thy praises
  For ever with the just.

Lord Jesus, bounteous giver
  Of light and life divine,
Thou didst my soul deliver;
  To thee I all resign.
Thou hast in mercy bought me
  With blood and bitter pain;
Let me, since thou hast sought me,
  Eternal life obtain.
—506 SBH, 334 LH

PRAYER

Dear heavenly Father: Help me never to steal money from others by doing poor work or loafing on the job. In Jesus' name. Amen. The Lord's Prayer.

Thursday   *The Seventh Commandment*

". . . so that we do not take our neighbor's . . . property."

People sometimes feel that they have a right to steal from someone who has more than they have. But if it is right for one person to take what belongs to another, it is right for everyone to do so. I may think the next fellow has more theme paper than he needs, but someone else may think that I have more than I need. That is why God made each person's property a sacred thing. If it were not, society could not go on. Private property means more than simply things we can see and touch. Ideas are private property, and we can steal them just as well as we can steal our neighbor's garden hose. Whenever we copy another person's work in school, we are stealing from him. If we copy his essay, we are stealing his ideas. If we copy his answers to arithmetic problems, we are stealing the energy and thought he put in on them. A Christian must ask himself, "What would happen if everyone did what I am doing?"

The Bible says that if we love others we will not break the Commandments:

> Owe no one anything, except to love one another; for he who loves his neighbor has fulfilled the law. Love does no wrong to a neighbor; therefore love is the fulfilling of the law.
>
> —Romans 13:8 and 10

In the following hymn we have good advice and encouragement for living the Christian life:

> *Fight the good fight with all thy might,*
> *Christ is thy strength, and Christ thy right;*
> *Lay hold on life, and it shall be*
> *Thy joy and crown eternally.*
>
> *Run the straight race through God's good grace,*
> *Lift up thine eyes, and seek his face;*
> *Life with its way before us lies,*
> *Christ is the path, and Christ the prize.*
>
> —557 SBH, 447 LH

PRAYER

Dear heavenly Father: Help me to respect the property of others and to be satisfied with what I can get by fair and honest ways. In Jesus' name. Amen. The Lord's Prayer.

". . . but help him to improve and protect his property and means of making a living."

Luther shows us that every Commandment that tells us not to do something also means that there is something we should do. The Seventh Commandment tells us not to steal our neighbor's money or property. But it is not enough that we just don't steal it. God wants us to help our neighbor to add to his money and to make his property worth more. The world could not get along if people only did not do certain things. People must also do things; they must help each other.

People on farms often help each other with threshing, fence-building, barn-raising, and the like. You will have a chance to give your friend a lift with the screens, or the lawn, or washing the car. When our neighbor goes away on vacation, we have a fine opportunity to help improve his property by keeping his lawn cut and trimmed until he returns. God expects us to be good, helpful neighbors.

If we followed Jesus' command, we would want to help our neighbor improve his property as though it were our own. Jesus said:

> You shall love the Lord your God with all your heart, and with all your soul, and with all your strength, and with all your mind; and your neighbor as yourself.
>
> —Luke 10:27

In this hymn we offer ourselves to God in his service, which must always mean the service of other people:

> *Take my life, and let it be*
> *Consecrated, Lord, to thee;*
> *Take my moments and my days,*
> *Let them flow in ceaseless praise.*
>
> *Take my hands, and let them move*
> *At the impulse of thy love;*
> *Take my feet, and let them be*
> *Swift and beautiful for thee.*
>
> —510 SBH, 400 LH

PRAYER

Dear heavenly Father: Help me to want the best for my neighbor's property, as for my own. In Jesus' name. Amen. The Lord's Prayer.

Saturday   *The Seventh Commandment*

". . . but help him to improve and protect his property and means of making a living."

A vandal is one who damages or destroys the property of others. Every now and then a wave of vandalism occurs in our cities; tires are slashed, windows broken, and public property damaged. Most of the time this is done by gangs of teen-agers who have not been taught the Seventh Commandment and its explanation by their parents or the church. So the policemen have to be the protectors of our property and arrest those who violate the Seventh Commandment. It would be much better if we would respect and protect each other's property.

Jesus gives us advice we should always remember as a guide to our actions:

> So whatever you wish that men would do to you, do so to them; for this is the law and the prophets.
>
> —Matthew 7:12

The following hymn asks God for strength to help our neighbor:

> *In sickness, sorrow, want, or care,*
> *Whate'er it be, 'tis ours to share;*
> *May we, where help is needed, there*
> *Give help as unto thee.*
>
> *And may thy Holy Spirit move*
> *All those who live, to live in love,*
> *Till thou shalt greet in heaven above*
> *All those who live to thee.*
>
> 316 SBH

PRAYER

Dear heavenly Father: Help me to want to respect and protect my neighbor's property as though it were mine. In Jesus' name. Amen. The Lord's Prayer.

Sunday   *The Eighth Commandment*

"You shall not bear false witness against your neighbor."

We have said that we ought to consider our neighbor's property as if it were our own and help him to improve and protect it. Part of our neighbor's property is his reputation—what others think of him. To many men, their reputation is their most valuable property. Think of how important the right kind of reputation is to a doctor or lawyer or businessman. All of us have our own reputations. We all want others to think and say the very best about us. We could not bear to go through life having our neighbors and friends thinking and speaking evil of us. Yet many reputations are wrecked by "false witness"—by lies and gossip, which people are always more ready to hear than the truth. Just one false word on your part may get the whole class at school whispering nasty things about John or Mary and may even cause them to leave school. That is why God wants us to help our neighbor improve and protect his reputation as though it were our own.

St. James tells us how our tongues can cause trouble:

> And the tongue is a fire. The tongue is an unrighteous world among our members, staining the whole body, setting on fire the cycle of nature, and set on fire by hell. For every kind of beast and bird, of reptile and sea creature, can be tamed and has been tamed by humankind, but no human being can tame the tongue—a restless evil, full of deadly poison.
>
> —James 3:6-8

We ask Jesus in the following hymn to help us to be truthful:

> *Lead us, O Father, in the paths of truth;*
> *Unhelped by thee, in error's maze we grope,*
> *While passion stains and folly dims our youth,*
> *And age comes on, uncheered by faith or hope.*
>
> *Lead us, O Father, in the paths of right;*
> *Blindly we stumble when we walk alone,*
> *Involved in shadows of a darkening night;*
> *Only with thee we journey safely on.*
>
> —472 SBH

PRAYER

Dear Lord Jesus: Help me to control my tongue, and to speak only the truth about others. Amen. The Lord's Prayer.

"... so that we do not betray ... our neighbor ..."

To betray someone means to break the confidence and trust he has in you. One of the worst things that happened in World War II was that people betrayed each other. High officials betrayed their countries and handed them over to the Nazis. Many others in high places betrayed the trust their people had put in them and turned their governments over to the Communists. In Germany and China and Russia, sons and daughters betrayed their own parents and each other and their neighbors to the secret police. Our society cannot exist very long if people cannot trust in and depend on one another for love and understanding and protection. If someone has put his trust and confidence in you, you have a sacred duty to keep that trust and not to let your friend down.

The worst example in all history of a person's betraying his friend is that of Judas' betrayal of Jesus:

> Then one of the twelve, who was called Judas Iscariot, went to the chief priests and said, "What will you give me if I deliver him to you?" And they paid him thirty pieces of silver. And from that moment he sought an opportunity to betray him.
>
> —Matthew 26:14-16

In this hymn we admit that we need Jesus to save us from our sinful thoughts and words towards others:

> *Just as I am, without one plea,*
> *But that thy Blood was shed for me,*
> *And that thou bidd'st me come to thee,*
> *O Lamb of God, I come, I come.*

> *Just as I am, and waiting not*
> *To rid my soul of one dark blot,*
> *To thee, whose Blood can cleanse each spot,*
> *O Lamb of God, I come, I come.*
> —370 SBH, 388 LH

PRAYER

Dear Lord Jesus: Help me never to betray anyone who loves me or puts trust in me. Amen. The Lord's Prayer.

Tuesday *The Eighth Commandment*

"... so that we do not ... slander ... our neighbor ..."

To slander someone is to say something purposely about him that will hurt his name or reputation. A lot of slandering goes on in political campaigns! What we say may or may not be true—the point is that we say it because we *want* to hurt that person. Sometimes we slander in order to get even for something said about us; sometimes we do it out of jealousy toward our class-mate who gets higher grades than we do, or because we resent a neighbor who keeps his lawn in better shape than we do ours.

But no matter why we try to harm others by slandering them, it shows that we need more of Jesus' love for other people, more of his forgiveness and more honesty to confess our own sins and shortcomings.

Jesus gives us some advice that will keep us from slandering others if we put it into practice:

> Why do you see the speck that is in your brother's eye, but do not notice the log that is in your own eye? Or how can you say to your brother, "Let me take the speck out of your eye," when there is the log in your own eye? You hypocrite, first take the log out of your own eye, and then you will see clearly to take the speck out of your brother's eye.
>
> —Mattthew 7:3-5

In this hymn we ask God to take away wickedness from our hearts:

> *Search me, God, and know my heart,*
>   *Lord of truth and mercy;*
> *Try me, thou who from afar*
>   *Knowest all my secrets;*
> *And if any wicked way*
>   *Should be found within me,*
> *Blessed Saviour, lead thou me*
>   *In the way eternal.*
>
> —378 SBH

PRAYER

Dear Lord Jesus: May I never say anything about others that I would not want them to say about me. Amen. The Lord's Prayer.

Wednesday   *The Eighth Commandment*

"... so that we do not ... lie about our neighbor ..."

"I didn't break the window—David did!" Sometimes we are tempted to lie about others in order to put the blame on them for something we said or did. This is done every day by children who want to escape being punished by their parents, and by grownups in court who try to escape fines or imprisonment.

Two wrongs never make a right. God expects us to be honest enough to confess our wrongs and not try to put the blame on others by lying.

St. Paul reminds us of our Christian responsibilities toward each other:

> Therefore, putting away falsehood, let every one speak the truth with his neighbor, for we are members one of another.
>
> —Ephesians 4:25

One of the most beautiful hymns of the Christian Church asks Jesus to heal our sinful natures:

> *Dear Lord and Father of mankind,*
> *Forgive our foolish ways;*
> *Reclothe us in our rightful mind,*
> *In purer lives thy service find,*
> *In deeper reverence praise.*
>
> *Breathe through the heats of our desire*
> *Thy coolness and thy balm;*
> *Let sense be dumb, let flesh retire;*
> *Speak through the earthquake, wind, and fire,*
> *O still small voice of calm!*
>
> —467 SBH

PRAYER

Dear Lord Jesus: Give me the courage to own up to the wrong I have done. Amen. The Lord's Prayer.

"... but defend him ..."

When we apologize for someone or "defend" him, we try to "fix things up for him," as we say. Doing that can be either good or bad. It is bad when dishonest politicians "fix" things for crooks and get them off with short jail sentences or a small fine. That is simply protecting and encouraging evil.

But when someone we know has done something wrong for which he is sorry, or has gotten into trouble by accident, he needs our help in explaining things or defending him. Or perhaps someone at a dinner party is embarrassed by spilling food or dropping silverware or breaking a dish. Instead of being one of those who laugh and snicker, you should be the one who says something that will make the person who had the accident feel that he or she has at least one friend who understands and is trying to help. That is what God expects us to do as a part of helping our neighbor, just as we would like to be helped by him.

The greatest example we have in all history of apologizing for our neighbor is Christ when he prayed for those who crucified him:

> And Jesus said, "Father, forgive them; for they know not what they do."
>
> —Luke 23:34

This hymn reminds us that on our own we are not strong enough to think and speak and act as we ought:

> *Rock of Ages, cleft for me,*
> *Let me hide myself in thee;*
> *Let the water and the blood,*
> *From thy riven side which flowed,*
> *Be of sin the double cure,*
> *Cleanse me from its guilt and power.*
>
> *Not the labors of my hands*
> *Can fulfill thy law's demands;*
> *Could my zeal no respite know,*
> *Could my tears for ever flow,*
> *All for sin could not atone;*
> *Thou must save, and thou alone.*
>
> —379 SBH, 376 LH

PRAYER

Dear Lord Jesus. Help me to follow your example and defend others whenever I can. Amen. The Lord's Prayer.

Friday   *The Eighth Commandment*

"... but ... speak well of him ..."

One very simple test we can make to see if we are putting our Christian faith into practice is to ask ourselves how many times we have said something good about someone else. It would be hard for most of us to remember the last time we did! On the other hand, all of us can remember quite a few things we said about others that were not so good.

The devil sees to it that we just naturally run other people down, but we have to try awfully hard to think of nice things to say about them, even when they deserve it. For instance, we play and work with our best friends day in and day out, but how often do we compliment them or say anything good about them? Do we ever tell anyone what fine friends, what kind, loving parents, or what patient and understanding teachers we have? Others need such words of praise and encouragement just as much as we do ourselves. Such words are the oil that makes the machinery of life run smoothly; and sometimes such words are the very fuel itself, without which the machinery would not run at all.

Jesus spoke well of people. For instance, this is what he said of the centurion who asked him to heal his servant:

> When Jesus heard him, he marveled, and said to those who followed him, "Truly, I say to you, not even in Israel have I found such faith."
>
> —Matthew 8:10

We confess our sinful natures in this hymn and ask God's help to be better:

> *Lord Jesus, think on me,*
> *And purge away my sin;*
> *From earth-born passions set me free,*
> *And make me pure within.*
>
> *Lord Jesus, think on me,*
> *Nor let me go astray;*
> *Through darkness and perplexity*
> *Point thou the heavenly way.*
> —365 SBH, 320 LH

PRAYER

Dear Lord Jesus: Help me to protect and build up my neighbor's reputation by speaking well of him whenever I possibly can. Amen. The Lord's Prayer.

59

". . . and explain his actions in the kindest way."

It is very easy to jump to conclusions about what people do, before we really find out the facts. It seems to be a kind of indoor sport for us to imagine all the evil reasons behind John's or Mary's doing such or such a thing when, actually, there might be a very good and Christian reason for their doing it.

When we don't know the facts, we should always think and believe the best about others, instead of the worst. If we see one of our classmates talking to the teacher after school, we shouldn't jump to the conclusion that he is "polishing the apple." If a policeman rings our neighbor's doorbell, we shouldn't begin to wonder what terrible things are going on. We should always "explain in the kindest way" what we see and hear.

Jesus reminds us:

> Judge not, that you be not judged. For with the judgment you pronounce you will be judged, and the measure you give will be the measure you get.
>
> —Matthew 7:1-2

We ask Jesus in this hymn to inspire us to live better Christian lives:

> *My faith looks up to thee,*
> *Thou Lamb of Calvary,*
> *Saviour divine!*
> *Now hear me while I pray,*
> *Take all my guilt away,*
> *O let me from this day*
> *Be wholly thine.*
>
> *May thy rich grace impart*
> *Strength to my fainting heart,*
> *My zeal inspire;*
> *As thou hast died for me,*
> *O may my love to thee,*
> *Pure, warm, and changeless be,*
> *A living fire.*
>
> —375 SBH, 394 LH

PRAYER

Dear Lord Jesus: Help me always to think the best of my neighbor's words and actions. Amen. The Lord's Prayer.

Sunday   *The Ninth and Tenth Commandments*

"You shall not covet."

To covet means to want what belongs to another person. It means that you are jealous because he has something you don't have and which you would take away from him if you could. There have always been covetous people, but today there are more things to covet than ever before. Scientists and inventors and manufacturers work night and day to turn out more and more things, and magazines and newspapers and radios and TVs work night and day to make us want all these things.

We see the beautiful colored advertisements of cars and clothes and houses, and we want them for ourselves. We are unhappy because some people can afford these things when we can't. Being covetous takes the joy out of life. Our desire for more and more things is making slaves of all of us and taking us away from God. If we put God first, rather than things, he has promised that he will take care of all our needs:

> Therefore do not be anxious, saying, "What shall we eat?" or "What shall we drink?" or "What shall we wear?" . . . But seek first his kingdom and his righteousness, and all these things shall be yours as well.
> —Matthew 6:31 and 33

In this hymn we sing about things that all of us have and can be thankful for:

> *For the beauty of the earth,*
> *For the beauty of the skies,*
> *For the love which from our birth*
> *Over and around us lies,*
> *Christ, our God, to thee we raise*
> *This our sacrifice of praise.*
>
> *For the beauty of each hour*
> *Of the day and of the night,*
> *Hill and vale, and tree and flower,*
> *Sun and moon and stars of light,*
> *Christ, our God, to thee we raise*
> *This our sacrifice of praise.*
> —444 SBH

PRAYER

Dear heavenly Father: Help me to love you above all things of the world and to do your will. In Jesus' name. Amen. The Lord's Prayer.

Monday   *The Ninth and Tenth Commandments*

"You shall not covet."

After World War II many of our soldiers wanted to get married and begin a home and family. But there were not enough houses. Many newly-married couples spent days and weeks looking for a place to live. There was a picture in a newspaper of one couple with several small children who spent the night in a railroad station. In some areas there is still a housing shortage. Here and there you will see that families are living in the basements of their unfinished homes. How easy it is, under such conditions, for people to covet other people's houses—to be envious of those who enjoy warm, comfortable homes!

Even if our family does have its own home, our neighbor may have a bigger, finer one—the kind we have always dreamed of living in.

But a house alone does not make a home; it takes love and work, and it takes God. Instead of coveting our neighbor's *house*, God wants us to be happy where we are and try to make it a *home*.

Jesus tells how being covetous ruins a person spiritually:

> And others are the ones sown among thorns; they are those who hear the word, but the cares of the world, and the delight in riches, and the desire for other things, enter in and choke the word, and it proves unfruitful.
>
> —Mark 4:18-19

In the words of the following hymn we thank God for the blessings of home and family;

> *For the joy of human love,*
> *Brother, sister, parent, child,*
> *Friends on earth and friends above,*
> *For all gentle thoughts and mild,*
> *Christ, our God, to thee we raise*
> *This our sacrifice of praise.*
>
> —444 SBH

PRAYER

Dear heavenly Father: Help me not to be jealous of other people's houses, but to love my own home and family. In Jesus' name. Amen. The Lord's Prayer.

Tuesday   *The Ninth and Tenth Commandments*

"You shall not covet."

We have talked about coveting our neighbor's house. It is also possible to covet his home. The word "home" includes house, family, possessions, background, and so on. Perhaps you have heard the remark, "If I had come from a home like hers, I'd have done better too." Maybe that is true, and maybe it isn't. We know that many young people who come from what we call "good" homes do not turn out so well themselves. On the other hand, many of the world's greatest and most successful people have come from average or even very poor homes. God wants us to count our blessings and be sure that we are doing all that we can to make our home what he wants it to be, rather than to covet our friend's home and be unhappy with our own.

In spite of the fact that Jesus came from a poor home in a little country town, the Bible tells us:

> And Jesus increased in wisdom and in stature, and in favor with God and man.
>
> —Luke 2:52

In this hymn we say that it is God's blessings that matter most in our homes:

> *Now thank we all our God*
> *With heart and hands and voices,*
> *Who wondrous things hath done,*
> *In whom his world rejoices;*
> *Who, from our mother's arms,*
> *Hath blessed us on our way*
> *With countless gifts of love,*
> *And still is ours today.*
>
> —443 SBH, 36 LH

PRAYER

Dear heavenly Father: Help me to appreciate the blessings of my own home and family. In Jesus' name. Amen. The Lord's Prayer.

The Ninth and Tenth Commandments

"You shall not covet."

We live in an age of gadgets, or mechanical appliances. Science has produced thousands of these things supposedly to make life more comfortable and enjoyable. Instead, all of us are in a race for more and more gadgets; and the more we get, the more we want. We are never satisfied; we have all become covetous. There are millions of people in our country who have given up almost everything else in life, including children, in order to have a new car or fine furniture. Many people feel that life is not worth living unless they can have a television set. Mary is unhappy because Joan has her own TV in her room and Mary doesn't. We are so covetous of things that we go deeply into debt in order to buy them.

Real happiness is inside of us, and if we have happiness there, we will have it even though our neighbors have more and better things than we do. God wants our happiness to depend, not on things but on our love for him and his love for us.

Jesus tells us that our most precious possessions are not here on earth:

> Do not lay up for yourselves treasures on earth, where moth and rust consume and where thieves break in and steal, but lay up for yourselves treasures in heaven, where neither moth nor rust consumes and where thieves do not break in and steal. For where your treasure is, there will your heart be also.
> —Matthew 6:19-21

In this hymn we tell Jesus that he is our only source of true happiness.

> *Jesus, thou Joy of loving hearts,*
> *Thou Fount of life, thou Light of men,*
> *From the best bliss that earth imparts*
> *We turn unfilled to thee again.*
> *We taste thee, O thou living Bread,*
> *And long to feast upon thee still;*
> *We drink of thee, the Fountainhead,*
> *And thirst our souls from thee to fill.*
>
> —483 SBH

PRAYER

Dear heavenly Father: Help me to try to find happiness not in things, but in serving you. In Jesus' name. Amen. The Lord's Prayer.

Thursday   *The Ninth and Tenth Commandments*

"You shall not covet."

The real reason for having clothes is to protect our bodies, but looks seem to be the important thing. A few so-called fashion experts decide each year what the "new look" is going to be; then millions of people follow along, whether they really like it or not, for fear that they will be out of style. The clothing advertisements tell us that if we want to be popular, glamorous, successful, and confident, we must wear the latest fashions. If we cannot afford all the clothes we would like, we begin to covet the clothes others have.

No matter how many expensive clothes we wear, we cannot cover up what we really are. It is a real sin to covet expensive, showy clothes when millions of people in Europe and Asia have only rags to wear. Thousands of people actually freeze to death every winter because they have no clothes. God wants us to remember all those who do not have enough to wear, and to be thankful that we have good clothing to keep us warm and comfortable. Jesus asks:

> And why are you anxious about clothing? Consider the lilies of the field, how they grow; they neither toil nor spin; yet I tell you, even Solomon in all his glory was not arrayed like one of these. But if God so clothes the grass of the field, which today is alive and tomorrow is thrown into the oven, will he not much more clothe you, O men of little faith?
> —Matthew 6:28-30

Instead of being unhappy over what we do not have, we are encouraged by this hymn to praise God for the blessings we do have:

> *O Lord of heaven and earth and sea,*
> *To thee all praise and glory be;*
> *How shall we show our love to thee,*
>   *Who givest all?*

> *For peaceful homes and healthful days,*
> *For all the blessings earth displays,*
> *We owe thee thankfulness and praise,*
>   *Who givest all.*
>
> —448 SBH, 443 LH

PRAYER

Dear heavenly Father: Help me to think of all those who are poor and needy and to be thankful for the things I have. In Jesus' name. Amen. The Lord's Prayer.

                   The Ninth and Tenth Commandments

"You shall not covet."

Just as everyone is not born into the same kind of home, so everyone is not born with the same face and body and color of hair and eyes. There are great differences among people in their physical makeup. This fact makes many people unhappy and covetous of others' looks. Modern advertising and the movies set styles in looks as well as in clothes. Many girls feel that in order to be attractive they must look like models or movie stars, and boys wish they were six feet tall with broad shoulders, like the men in the magazines and on the screen.

If we are jealous or covetous of someone we think is better looking than we are, we should remember that it is our personality that counts most with others, and personality does not depend on looks. God wants you to be a real person, and your appearance will take care of itself.

St. Paul says that the important thing is to give ourselves to God:

> I appeal to you therefore, brethren, by the mercies of God, to present your bodies as a living sacrifice, holy and acceptable to God, which is your spiritual worship.
> —Romans 12:1

We offer ourselves to God in the words of this hymn:

> *Take my life, and let it be*
> *Consecrated, Lord, to thee;*
> *Take my moments and my days,*
> *Let them flow in ceaseless praise.*
>
> *Take my hands, and let them move*
> *At the impulse of thy love;*
> *Take my feet, and let them be*
> *Swift and beautiful for thee.*
> —510 SBH, 400 LH

PRAYER

Dear heavenly Father: Help me to make the best possible use of the body you have given me. In Jesus' name. Amen. The Lord's Prayer.

"You shall not covet."

Some of us may be unhappy because we feel that we are not as smart as others we know. Although we should always try to improve our minds by study and practice, we must try to understand that all of us cannot be equally good in all things, and that there is plenty of room and need in the world for all kinds of minds. Winston Churchill could not pass his Latin course.

If we cannot work as fast as others, that is not necessarily bad either. Many scientists and scholars are very slow workers, and people who are fast often have to do their work over again. God expects you to make the best possible use of your mind.

If we dedicate our minds to God, we will make good use of them:

> . . . and you shall love the Lord your God with all your heart, and with all your soul, and with all your mind, and with all your strength.
> —Mark 12:30

In this hymn we offer our minds to God:

> *Take my silver and my gold,*
> *Not a mite would I withhold;*
> *Take my intellect, and use*
> *Every power as thou shalt choose.*
>
> *Take my will and make it thine,*
> *It shall be no longer mine;*
> *Take my heart, it is thine own,*
> *It shall be thy royal throne.*
> —510 SBH, 400 LH

PRAYER

Dear heavenly Father: Help me to make the best use possible of the mind you have given me. In Jesus' name. Amen. The Lord's Prayer.

Sunday   *Conclusion to the Commandments*

"I, the Lord your God, am a jealous God . . ."

There is a good way to be jealous. For example, we ought to be jealous of the freedom we enjoy in our country; we should guard it and not let anyone take it away from us. We ought to be jealous of our church, and do everything we can to make it better and more Christian. God is jealous of his people whom he has created. He does not want us to come under the power of the devil. He wants us to fear, love, and trust in him above all things. He wants us to do it for our own good and because it is the only way we can really be happy. God is so jealous of his people—he loves us so much and he wants so much to keep us for himself—that he sent his only Son into the world to save us from our sins and from the devil.

One of the best-known and loved Bible verses puts it this way:

> For God so loved the world that he gave his only Son, that whoever believes in him should not perish but have eternal life.
>
> —John 3:16

This hymn reminds us of how much God wants us for his own:

> *He suffered shame and scorn,*
> *And wretched, dire disgrace;*
> *Forsaken and forlorn,*
> *He hung there in our place.*
> *But such as would from sin be free*
> *Look to his Cross for victory.*
>
> *His life, his all, he gave*
> *When he was crucified;*
> *Our burdened souls to save,*
> *What fearful death he died!*
> *But each of us, though dead in sin,*
> *Through him eternal life may win.*
>
> —80 SBH

PRAYER

Dear heavenly Father: Help me to fear, love, and trust in you above all things. In Jesus' name. Amen. The Lord's Prayer.

". . . visiting the iniquity . . ."

"Visiting the iniquity" really means that when we do what is sinful, we bring trouble on ourselves and on other innocent people. When you light a match near a gasoline can, you're going to get hurt. Just as surely, when you disobey God's moral laws, you will hurt yourself and probably others. You can say that God punishes us when we do wrong, but you can also say that we punish ourselves.

This Bible verse tells us that God does not want us to sin but to be saved:

> For God has not destined us for wrath, but to obtain salvation through our Lord Jesus Christ, who died for us so that whether we wake or sleep we might live with him.
> —1 Thessalonians 5:9-10

In this hymn we admit we deserve God's anger, but we beg his forgiveness and help:

> *Smite us not in anger, Lord,*
> *But in mercy spare us,*
> *Save us from our just reward,*
> *In Thy pity hear us.*
> *Though our sin,*
> *Great hath been,*
> *Let Christ's intercession*
> *Cover our transgression.*
>
> *Strengthen us in love, O Lord,*
> *Gently as a Father;*
> *When Thou dost Thy help afford*
> *All our fears are over.*
> *Weak indeed,*
> *We have need*
> *That Thy love correct us,*
> *And Thy grace protect us.*
> —313 CSB

PRAYER

Dear heavenly Father: Help me to obey your commandments and to fight against the devil and all his works and ways. In Jesus' name. Amen. The Lord's Prayer.

Tuesday   *Conclusion to the Commandments*

". . . visiting the iniquity of the fathers upon the children . . ."

"Visiting the iniquity of the fathers upon the children" means that God punishes children for the sins of their parents. One generation suffers for the sins of another. At first, this may seem very unfair. But we see it going on all around us, and when we think about it, we see that it could not be any other way. If parents do things that are wrong, their children will do them too and get into trouble. If parents break up their homes by divorce, the children certainly suffer in many ways. When people ruin their health before marriage, their children often must go through life with bad health and diseased bodies. As long as people sin, innocent people will suffer. That is what makes sin so awful. If only the ones who sinned had to suffer, sin would not be so terrible, but innocent ones pay the price too. So we have not only ourselves to think of, but others who will suffer for our sins: our friends, our families, and our children.

God wants parents to bring their children to him by good example and warns them of the dangers of setting a bad example:

> . . . but whoever causes one of these little ones who believe in me to sin, it would be better for him to have a great millstone fastened round his neck and to be drowned in the depth of the sea.
>
> —Matthew 18:6

We commit our children to Jesus' care in the following hymn:

> *Lead every child that bears thy Name*
> *To walk in thine own guileless way,*
> *To dread the touch of sin and shame,*
> *And humbly, like thyself, obey.*
>
> *So shall they waiting here below,*
> *Like thee their Lord, a little span,*
> *In wisdom and in stature grow,*
> *And favor with both God and man.*
>
> —334 SBH

PRAYER

Dear heavenly Father: Help me to obey your commandments so that I may not be a bad example to others or cause them to do wrong. In Jesus' name. Amen. The Lord's Prayer.

Wednesday   *Conclusion to the Commandments*

". . . to the third and fourth generation . . ."

It is a terrifying lesson to see how God's warning comes true that people's sins harm children three and four generations away: their great-grandchildren. We can see that bad morals are handed down from generation to generation. Perhaps a person makes a will in a moment of anger or selfishness which cuts out certain members of his family from their inheritance and makes them poor. Think how many children have suffered and will suffer because of wars which their parents and grandparents brought about. It is impossible to tell how far a sinful word or act of ours will go, and how many other people it will harm. God tells us to follow him and obey his commandments so that we will be able to help others rather than harm them.

Jesus says that God holds us responsible for what happens to others because of our sins:

> Woe to the world for temptations to sin! For it is necessary that temptations come, but woe to the man by whom the temptation comes!
>
> —Matthew 18:7

This hymn praises the Christians of the past whose faith inspires us today:

> *Faith of our fathers! living still*
> *In spite of dungeon, fire, and sword;*
> *O how our hearts beat high with joy*
> *Whene'er we hear that glorious word:*
> *Faith of our fathers, holy faith,*
> *We will be true to thee till death.*
>
> *Our fathers, chained in prisons dark,*
> *Were still in heart and conscience free,*
> *And blest would be their children's fate,*
> *If they, like them, should die for thee:*
> *Faith of our fathers, holy faith,*
> *We will be true to thee till death.*
>
> —516 SBH

PRAYER

Dear heavenly Father: Help me feel responsible for every word and action and to think of how it may help or harm someone else. In Jesus' name. Amen. The Lord's Prayer.

71

Thursday   *Conclusion to the Commandments*

". . . to the third and fourth generation of those who hate me . . ."

We all know what the word hate means, but we have a hard time believing that anyone would hate God. We know that all people sin. Some disobey him more than others, but we say, "Being disobedient to God is no sign that you hate him." This statement implies that we do not understand how sin and the devil work. No person would come to hate God by himself, but the devil gets us to love doing what is wrong more and more, until we hate anything and anybody, including God, that might stop us. Most children have actually hated their parents at some time or other for stopping them from doing something bad that they wanted very much to do. This is the trick that sin plays on us: it gets us to hate the very things that are good for us. The more we sin, the harder it is not to. That is why we should begin now, this very day, to obey God's commandments.

This is what St. Paul advises in our struggles with Satan:

> Finally, be strong in the Lord and in the strength of his might. Put on the whole armor of God, that you may be able to stand against the wiles of the devil.
>
> —Ephesians 6:10-11

Here is a hymn that says how much God wants us to love and follow him:

> *Jesus calls us; o'er the tumult*
> *Of our life's wild, restless sea,*
> *Day by day his clear voice soundeth,*
> *Saying, "Christian, follow me!"*
>
> *Jesus calls us! By thy mercies,*
> *Saviour, make us hear thy call,*
> *Give our hearts to thine obedience,*
> *Serve and love thee best of all.*
> —553 SBH, 270 LH

PRAYER

Dear heavenly Father: Help me to be strong enough to stand against temptation. Help me to love you and to hate evil. In Jesus' name. Amen. The Lord's Prayer.

Friday   *Conclusion to the Commandments*

"... but showing steadfast love to thousands of those who love me ..."

From the very beginning of the human race, criminals have asked for mercy from those who held the power of life and death over them. The man who commits a crime wants the judge to have pity on him and give him another chance. When we sin against God we commit crime and deserve punishment. But God is always ready to have mercy on us if we are truly sorry and want to obey him. It makes our heavenly Father very sorrowful when we do not want his mercy and continue in our sinful ways. God's wish is that all people should be his children, love him and live according to his commandments.

St. Peter reminds us of God's great mercy:

> The Lord is not slow about his promise as some count slowness, but is forbearing toward you, not wishing that any should perish, but that all should reach repentance.
> —2 Peter 3:9

We sing of God's mercy in this favorite hymn:

> *There's a wideness in God's mercy,*
> *Like the wideness of the sea;*
> *There's a kindness in his justice,*
> *Which is more than liberty.*
>
> *For the love of God is broader*
> *Than the measures of man's mind,*
> *And the heart of the Eternal*
> *Is most wonderfully kind.*
> —493 SBH

PRAYER

Dear heavenly Father: Help me to be sorry for my sins and thankful for your love and mercy to me. In Jesus' name. Amen. The Lord's Prayer.

"... who love me and keep my commandments."

Notice that God says he will show mercy to those who love him and keep his commandments. That makes it impossible for us to say we love God, without doing something about it. If we love our parents we don't only tell them about it, but we try also to help them with the work around the house. We remember them with gifts on their birthdays and at Christmas. We do something to show our love for them.

We must also do something about our love for God. We must try to obey his commandments, to live a pure life, and to love one another. It comes down to this: Christianity is more than talk. It is a way of life.

Jesus doesn't leave much doubt on this subject when he says:

> Not every one who says to me, "Lord, Lord," shall enter the kingdom of heaven, but he who does the will of my Father who is in heaven.
>
> —Matthew 7:21

In this hymn we ask God to help us do his will:

> *Jesus, Master, whom I serve,*
>   *Though so feebly and so ill,*
> *Strengthen hand and heart and nerve*
>   *All thy bidding to fulfill;*
> *Open thou mine eyes to see*
> *All the work thou hast for me.*
>
> *Jesus, Master, I am thine;*
>   *Keep me faithful, keep me near;*
> *Let thy presence in me shine*
>   *All my homeward way to cheer.*
> *Jesus, at thy feet I fall,*
> *O be thou my all in all.*
>
> —507 SBH

PRAYER

Dear heavenly Father: Help me to show by my actions as well as my words that I am a follower of yours. In Jesus' name. Amen. The Lord's Prayer.

PART TWO

The Apostles' Creed

THE FIRST ARTICLE

I believe in God the Father almighty, Maker of heaven and earth.

What does this mean?

I believe that God has created me
 and all that exists.
He has given me and still preserves
my body and soul with all their
 powers.

He provides me with food and clothing,
 home and family, daily work,
 and all I need from day to day.
God also protects me in time of danger
 and guards me from every evil.

All this he does out of fatherly and
 divine goodness and mercy,
 though I do not deserve it.
Therefore I surely ought to thank and
 praise, serve and obey him.

This is most certainly true.

THE SECOND ARTICLE

And in Jesus Christ his only Son, our Lord; who was conceived by the Holy Ghost, born of the Virgin Mary; suffered under Pontius Pilate, was crucified, dead, and buried; he descended into hell; the third day he rose again from the dead; he ascended into heaven, and sitteth on the right hand of God the Father almighty; from thence he shall come to judge the quick and the dead.

What does this mean?

I believe that Jesus Christ—
true God, Son of the Father from
eternity,
and true man, born of the Virgin Mary—
is my Lord.

He has redeemed me,
a lost and condemned person,
saved me at great cost
from sin, death, and the power of the
devil—

not with silver or gold,
but with his holy and precious blood
and his innocent suffering and death.

All this he has done that I may be his own,
live under him in his kingdom,
and serve him in everlasting righteousness, innocence, and blessedness,
just as he is risen from the dead and
lives and rules eternally.

This is most certainly true.

THE THIRD ARTICLE

I believe in the Holy Ghost; the holy Christian church, the communion of saints; the forgiveness of sins; the resurrection of the body; and the life everlasting. Amen.

What does this mean?

I believe that I cannot by my own
   understanding or effort
believe in Jesus Christ my Lord,
   or come to him.

But the Holy Spirit has called me
   through the Gospel,
enlightened me with his gifts,
and sanctified and kept me in true faith.

In the same way he calls, gathers,
   enlightens, and sanctifies
the whole Christian church on earth,
and keeps it united with Jesus Christ
   in the one true faith.

In this Christian church day after day
he fully forgives my sins
and the sins of all believers.

On the last day he will raise me and all
   the dead
and give me and all believers in Christ
   eternal life.

This is most certainly true.

"I believe in God the Father almighty, Maker of heaven and earth."

The Hebrews who wrote the Psalms and the Book of Genesis could not look at the earth or the sky without thinking how wonderful God was because he had made it all. We who live some 3,000 years after those writers ought to think that God is even more wonderful, because we know more about his creation than people ever knew before. Our telescopes have shown us that the heavens are full of countless millions of other worlds and suns, stretching out for millions of miles in all directions. Our microscopes have shown us that the world is full of all kinds of life that is too tiny for our naked eyes to see. The more we find out about the heavens and the earth, the more we see how perfectly everything has been planned and made and kept going, the more we should worship and praise God, who is the Creator of all things.

Here is one of the many Psalms that praise God, the Creator:

O give thanks to the Lord of lords,
    for his steadfast love endures for ever;
to him who by understanding made the heavens,
    for his steadfast love endures for ever;
to him who spread out the earth upon the waters,
    for his steadfast love endures for ever.

—Psalm 136:3, 5 and 6

In this hymn we praise God, the Creator:

Praise the Lord of heaven,
   Praise him in the height,
Praise him, all ye angels,
   Praise him, stars and light;
Praise him, clouds and waters,
   Which above the skies,
When his word commanded,
   Stablished did arise.

Praise the Lord, ye fountains
   Of the deeps and seas,
Rocks and hills and mountains,
   Cedars and all trees;
Praise him, clouds and vapors,
   Snow and hail and fire,
Stormy wind, fulfilling
   Only his desire.

—427 SBH

PRAYER

Dear heavenly Father: I praise and worship you as Creator of the heavens above and the earth on which I live. Help me to be thankful for these, your works. In Jesus' name. Amen. The Lord's Prayer.

                               The First Article

"I believe that God has created me ..."

It makes a lot of difference whether or not you believe God created you. If you believe, as some people do, that we just came into being by accident, or that we are simply a high type of animal, then you look at all of creation as an accident and yourself and others as animals. Then life doesn't make any sense and doesn't have any plan. There are so many people today who do not have a plan or a purpose in life, who are "all mixed up." The newspapers are full of things people do that are not only like, but far worse than, the things animals do.

But all that is changed when we believe that we are created by God, in his own image. That means that God put us here, not by accident, but for a purpose. It means that we cannot act and speak and think as though we were animals, but that we are to live as God's highest creation, according to his commandments for us. Man's high place in God's creation is spoken of by the psalmist:

> Yet thou hast made him little less than God,
>   and dost crown him with glory and honor.
> Thou hast given him dominion over the works of thy hands;
>   thou hast put all things under his feet.
>
> —Psalm 8:5-6

We praise God as our creator in this hymn:

> *The Lord, he is God, he hath made us, not we;*
>   *Glory be to God!*
> *The sheep of his pasture we evermore shall be;*
>   *Sing praise unto God out of Zion!*
>
> *O enter his gates with thanksgiving and praise;*
>   *Glory be to God!*
> *To honor his Name gladsome voices we will raise;*
>   *Sing praise unto God out of Zion!*
>
> —423 SBH

PRAYER

Dear heavenly Father: I praise and worship you as my Creator. Help me to live my life according to your purpose for me. In Jesus' name. Amen. The Lord's Prayer.

79

Tuesday   *The First Article*

"I believe that God has created . . . all that exists."

Today people think they can get along without God because they can make so many things for themselves. But we would not be able to make a single thing if God had not first made the raw materials. We could not build our skyscrapers if God had not first made the stone and the iron ore. We could not build our homes if God had not first made the trees grow for the wood and made the clay for the bricks. We could not even bake bread without the wheat that God makes grow for the flour. Everything that men make in factories and in shops is in turn made from things that come first from God. We really do not "make" anything. We simply change the shape or form of things that God has already created. We should recognize the hand of God in everything around us.

The psalmist saw the handiwork of God wherever he looked:

> In his hand are the depths of the earth;
>   the heights of the mountains are his also.
> The sea is his, for he made it;
>   for his hands formed the dry land.
>
> —Psalm 95:4-5

This hymn praises God as Creator of all things:

> *Dear mother earth, who day by day*
> *Unfoldest blessings on our way,*
>   *O praise him, alleluia!*
> *The flowers and fruits that in thee grow,*
> *Let them his glory also show:*
>   *O praise him, alleluia!*
>
> *Let all things their Creator bless,*
> *And worship him in humbleness;*
>   *O praise him, alleluia!*
> *Praise, praise the Father, praise the Son,*
> *And praise the Spirit, Three in One:*
>   *O praise him, alleluia!*
>
> —173 SBH

PRAYER

Dear heavenly Father: I praise and worship you as the Creator of all things. Help me to remember that every good thing comes from you. In Jesus' name. Amen. The Lord's Prayer.

"He has given me and still preserves my body . . ."

The human body is the most wonderful of all of God's physical creations. All through the ages, artists have considered the human body the most beautiful subject to paint and to sculpture in stone and wood. There is no machine that man has ever been able to make that can do the things that our bodies can do. Think of the hundreds of different kinds of work that people do with their arms and legs and hands and fingers and backs. Think of the swimming, running, archery, tennis, skating, and other sports our bodies make possible. Think how our bodies can fight off sickness, how they can repair themselves when injured, how they can adjust to great heat or cold, to water or to air. Only God could have planned and created the human body.

Christians believe the Bible when it says:

> So God created man in his own image, in the image of
> God he created him; male and female he created them.
> —Genesis 1:27

In this hymn we offer ourselves to God who made us:

> *God of our life, all-glorious Lord,*
> *Be now and evermore adored!*
> *Into the opening of this day*
> *Bring grace, and love, and peace, we pray.*
>
> *Give help for doing every task,*
> *Nor let us fail of thee to ask*
> *For grace in speech, for love in deed,*
> *From wrongful actions to be freed.*
>
> —209 SBH

PRAYER

Dear heavenly Father: I praise and worship you as the Creator of my body. Help me to keep it as your temple. In Jesus' name. Amen. The Lord's Prayer.

Thursday *The First Article*

"He has given me and still preserves my . . . soul."

We are more than just body; we are spirit, or soul, too. Our souls are our real selves. We use our bodies to move around in but they are merely "houses" for us to live in while we are in this world. When we think of a person, we think mostly of his personality, which is really another word for his spirit or his soul or the part that is his real self. Our souls are the part of us which God has made like himself, "in his own image." Our souls will live forever, and God has promised us new bodies for them after this life is over. There is an advertisement which says that a diamond is the most valuable gift because it lasts forever. That is why our souls are our most valuable possession, and we should thank God for them.

St. James tells us to protect our souls with the Word of God:

> Therefore put away all filthiness and rank growth of wickedness and receive with meekness the implanted word, which is able to save your souls.
>
> —James 1:21

Here is a hymn to the Maker of our souls:

> *O my soul, on wings ascending,*
> *On the holy mount seek rest,*
> *Where sweet angel-harps are blending*
> *With the anthems of the blest.*
> *Let thy fervent praise and prayer*
> *Come before thy Maker there,*
> *Knowing that, while yet a mortal,*
> *Thou art near the Father's portal.*
>
> *While upon this earth abiding,*
> *Let us never cease to pray,*
> *In the blessed Lord confiding,*
> *As our fathers in their day.*
> *Be the voice of children raised*
> *To the God our fathers praised;*
> *May his blessing, failing never,*
> *Rest on all his saints forever.*
>
> —462 SBH

PRAYER

Dear heavenly Father: I praise and worship you as the Creator of my soul. Help me to dedicate it to you. In Jesus' name. Amen. The Lord's Prayer.

                        The First Article

". . . my body and soul with all their powers."

Even though we often speak of our bodies and minds as being separate, our brains are actually part of our bodies, made out of tissues and kept alive by the bloodstream, just as the rest of the body is. When we think of the powers of the human brain, we realize that it is probably the greatest miracle of God's creation! It is through the powers of man's God-given mind that he has been able to make all the wonderful discoveries of the world and universe in which he lives and to control the forces of nature to serve him. It is through the powers of his mind that man is now beginning to conquer outer space and someday will travel to other planets.

But we must be humble about our brain-power because our sinful natures are always in danger of putting the powers of our minds to evil uses. That is why such discoveries as atomic power are mixed blessings. On the one hand, it can make possible a world of plenty for everyone, and on the other hand, it can be (and very well may be) used to blow the world to pieces. We should pray that God will give us the spiritual strength to use our minds to do his will.

Jesus said that the greatest commandment was:

> You shall love the Lord your God with all your heart, and with all your soul, and with all your mind.
> —Matthew 22:37

This hymn asks Jesus to rule over our minds:

> *O may that mind in us be formed*
> *Which shone so bright in Thee,*
> *An humble, meek, and lowly mind,*
> *From pride and envy free.*
>
> *May we to others stoop, and learn*
> *To emulate Thy love;*
> *So shall we bear Thine image here,*
> *And share Thy throne above.*
> —87 CSB

PRAYER

Dear heavenly Father: I praise and worship you as the Creator of my mind. Help me to use it to your glory and to the service of my fellow man. In Jesus' name. Amen. The Lord's Prayer.

Saturday   *The First Article*

". . . my body and soul with all their powers."

Too often we modern Christians are short on soul-power. We understand quite well how to develop the powers of our minds and bodies, but the kind of life we lead does not usually encourage us to develop the powers of the soul. To build up that kind of power we have to read our Bibles and think and pray about God's Word. We have to go through difficult experiences when God alone can help us. We have to work hard at putting into practice the things Jesus teaches us. But we are always trying to find the easy way out. We have so many material things to rely on and to make us safe and comfortable that many of us really don't feel the need to rely on God except when we become seriously ill or our material comforts are taken from us. This is why, in God's wisdom, he may from time to time allow us to go through difficulties of one kind or another so that we are forced to develop and exercise the powers of our souls.

This is the way St. Paul wants us to look at hardship when it comes:

> My son, do not regard lightly the discipline of the Lord, nor lose courage when you are punished by him. For the Lord disciplines him whom he loves, and chastises every son whom he receives . . . he disciplines us for our good, that we may share his holiness. For the moment all discipline seems painful rather than pleasant; later it yields the peaceful fruit of righteousness to those who have been trained by it.
>
> —Hebrews 12:5-11

We remind ourselves in this hymn that we must discipline and develop our souls:

Awake, my soul, stretch every nerve,
  And press with vigor on;
A heavenly race demands thy zeal,
  And an immortal crown.

A cloud of witnesses around
  Hold thee in full survey;
Forget the steps already trod,
  And onward urge thy way.

—552 SBH

PRAYER

Dear heavenly Father: Help me to develop my spiritual self along with my mind and body so that I may live in your heavenly kingdom. In Jesus' name. Amen. The Lord's Prayer.

"He provides me with food . . ."

Most of us are in the habit of thinking that our food comes from the store. We simply go to the grocery and buy what we need. We pay the grocer, but hardly ever stop to thank God, who is the one from whom our food really comes. Neither the grocer nor the farmer could make one stalk of celery or a single potato. These must grow in the soil, and God alone provides both the soil and the growth.

So you do not and can not ever pay God for your food. He has given it as a gift, free to all men. If men are too selfish to give everyone his share, that is not God's fault, but ours. As Christians, we should always give thanks to God before meals, because our food is truly a gift from him. The Bible writers knew that God gives us our food:

> Thou crownest the year with thy bounty;
>   the tracks of thy chariot drip with fatness.
> The pastures of the wilderness drip,
>   the hills gird themselves with joy,
> the meadows clothe themselves with flocks,
>   the valleys deck themselves with grain,
>   they shout and sing together for joy.
> —Psalm 65:11-13

We thank God for our food in this hymn:

> *We plough the fields, and scatter*
>   *The good seed on the land,*
> *But it is fed and watered*
>   *By God's almighty hand;*
> *He sends the snow in winter,*
>   *The warmth to swell the grain,*
> *The breezes and the sunshine,*
>   *And soft refreshing rain.*
> *All good gifts around us*
>   *Are sent from heaven above,*
> *Then thank the Lord,*
>   *O thank the Lord,*
>   *For all his love.*
> —364 SBH

PRAYER

Dear heavenly Father: I thank you for the food you have given me. I pray that all people may have enough food to eat. Amen. The Lord's Prayer.

Monday   *The First Article*

"He provides me with . . . clothing . . ."

Usually we don't stop to think where our coats and pants and dresses and hats really come from. We simply go down to the store and buy our clothing. Some of us know what company makes our clothing, but that is about as far as it goes.

It was not so when our country was young. In those days, the woman of the house made the family's clothing. First she made her thread on the spinning wheel, from the wool of sheep or from flax or from cotton. Then she wove the thread on a loom to make the cloth. She and her family knew that their clothing really came from God, who provided the flax and the cotton and the wool.

God has provided enough such raw materials so that everyone could have all the clothing he needs. Many people in the world do not have enough clothes to wear because of the greed and selfishness of those who work against God and who want more than their share. God has given enough for everyone.

The Bible tells us that God has provided for all our needs:

> Thou openest thy hand,
>   thou satisfiest the desire of every living thing.
> The Lord is just in all his ways,
>   and kind in all his doings.
>
> —Psalm 145:16-17

This hymn praises God, who has created everything we need:

> *Praise to the Lord, the Almighty, the King of creation;*
> *O my soul, praise him, for he is thy health and salvation:*
>   *All ye who hear,*
>   *Now to his temple draw near;*
> *Joining in glad adoration.*
>
> —408 SBH, 39 LH

PRAYER

Dear heavenly Father: I thank you for the clothing you have given me. I pray that all people may have enough clothes to wear. Amen. The Lord's Prayer.

"He provides me with . . . home . . ."

Any family who tried to build a house after World War II knows how much trouble it was. There was even a movie on the difficulty of building a house—*Mr. Blandings Builds His Dream House.* Materials like lumber, cement, and pipe were very hard to get and very expensive. Carpenters who knew their trade were few and far between, and everything connected with the house, including the land on which it stood, was two and three times as expensive as it used to be.

How then can we say that we believe God gives us our house? We have made everything so complicated these days that we often lose the main point. All the people we have to deal with and all the bills we have to pay to have a house are simply the result of the way we have arranged things in our society. God has had nothing to do with that!

The early pioneers knew that it was God who made the trees grow from which they built their cabins. The wood, the glass, the iron, the bricks, the cement in our houses are all made from the raw materials God has given us. That is why we say that God has given us our homes.

This psalm reminds us not to forget God's blessings:

> Bless the Lord, O my soul;
> and all that is within me,
>   bless his holy name!
> Bless the Lord, O my soul,
>   and forget not all his benefits . . .
>   —Psalm 103:1-2

In one of our national anthems we sing of the natural resources God has given us:

> *My native country, thee,*
> *Land of the noble free,*
>   *Thy name I love;*
> *I love thy rocks and rills,*
> *Thy woods and templed hills;*
> *My heart with rapture thrills*
>   *Like that above.*
>   —360 SBH

PRAYER

Dear heavenly Father: I thank you for my house. I pray that all people may have a place to live. Amen. The Lord's Prayer.

Wednesday   *The First Article*

"He provides me with . . . family . . ."

The family is the oldest organization in the world, and the most important one. God intended us to live in such a way that our life would be centered around the family. It is in the family that we learn obedience; it is in the family that we learn service, cooperation, and sharing. It is in the family that we learn morals—what is right and wrong. It is there we first learn about God. When Luther wrote his Catechism he intended that it should be taught to the various members of the family by "the head of the family." Whenever families have broken up, society has broken up. The family holds the world together.

These days, when so many forces are at work to pull our families apart, we should do everything possible to make our families strong, like having daily devotions together. It is said that "The family that prays together stays together."

We learn from the Bible that the family is a sacred institution that comes from God:

> So God created man in his own image, in the image of God he created him; male and female he created them. And God blessed them, and God said to them, "Be fruitful and multiply, and fill the earth and subdue it; and have dominion over the fish of the sea and over the birds of the air and over every living thing that moves upon the earth."
> —Genesis 1:27-28

In this hymn we thank God for a Christian family:

> *O happy home, where thou art loved the dearest,*
> *Thou loving Friend, and Saviour of our race,*
> *And where among the guests there never cometh*
> *One who can hold such high and honored place.*
>
> *O happy home, where each one serves thee, lowly,*
> *Whatever his appointed work may be,*
> *Till every common task seems great and holy,*
> *When it is done, O Lord, as unto thee.*
> —336 SBH, 626 LH

PRAYER

Dear heavenly Father: I thank you for the family that I have. I pray that all families may be blessed. Amen. The Lord's Prayer.

Thursday   *The First Article*

"He provides me with . . . daily work . . ."

Work has almost come to be a bad word nowadays. For a long time now we have tried very hard to get shorter and shorter hours for workmen, and there have been so many labor-saving devices invented that there is a danger in some places that all the work will be done by machines and men will be out of jobs completely. The best way to sell something is to show that it is easy to use or makes some job easier.

And yet we need to work for our own good. If the day ever comes when we don't have to work at all, we will lose one of God's greatest blessings. Having work that must be done gives us a purpose in life, keeps us from becoming lazy and soft, and gives us a good feeling of pride when we do it well. We should thank God for whatever jobs we have to do and do them to the very best of our ability.

Timothy, a young pastor, is told by St. Paul to do a job as a minister that he can be proud of:

> Do your best to present yourself to God as one approved,
> a workman who has no need to be ashamed, rightly handling
> the word of truth.
>
> —2 Timothy 2:15

We should think of our work as service to God, as we sing in this hymn:

> *Jesus, Master, whom I serve,*
>   *Though so feebly and so ill,*
> *Strengthen hand and heart and nerve*
>   *All thy bidding to fulfill;*
> *Open thou mine eyes to see*
> *All the work thou hast for me.*
>
> —507 SBH

PRAYER

Dear heavenly Father: I thank you for the work I have to do. May I do it as a service to you. In Jesus' name. Amen. The Lord's Prayer.

"God also protects me in time of danger ..."

The President of the United States has bodyguards who follow him wherever he goes so that he will be protected from people who might want to harm him. As long as the President puts himself in the care of his bodyguards, they will protect him. But if, as some presidents have done, he tries to get away from them and travel alone, his guards cannot protect him.

If we put ourselves in God's care, he will protect us, but if we go our way and do not obey him, it is not fair to expect him to take care of us. Most people run to God when they are in trouble or danger, but never think of him otherwise. It is often too late then. The only way we can expect God's protection is by being truly sorry for our sins and seeking to do his will at all times.

The psalmist tells us that if we put our trust in God there is nothing to be afraid of:

> The Lord is my light and my salvation;
>   whom shall I fear?
> The Lord is the stronghold of my life;
>   of whom shall I be afraid?
>
> —Psalm 27:1

This hymn assures us of God's protection:

> *How firm a foundation, ye saints of the Lord,*
> *Is laid for your faith in his excellent word!*
> *What more can he say than to you he hath said,*
> *Who unto the Saviour for refuge have fled?*
>
> *'The soul that on Jesus hath leaned for repose*
> *I will not, I cannot desert to his foes;*
> *That soul, though all hell should endeavor to shake,*
> *I'll never, no never, no never forsake!'*
>
> —558 SBH, 427 LH

PRAYER

Dear heavenly Father: I thank you for your protection against danger. I pray that I might put my trust in you. Amen. The Lord's Prayer.

"... and guards me from every evil."

If you were put in the ring to fight the world's heavyweight champion, you could not possibly hope to win. You would simply be no match for him.

As long as we are in this world we have to fight against evil—against the power of the devil. And we are no match for him by ourselves, because we are only human beings, and he is superhuman. We need God on our side in order to win the fight against the devil. God guards us and protects our weak spots so that the devil cannot conquer us. But here too we must first put ourselves in God's hands—we must try to do his will—if we expect him to guard us from evil. If we go our own way, we leave ourselves "wide open" to Satan's attacks and we become weaker and weaker and less able to fight.

By going regularly to church and Sunday school and Luther League, and by having daily devotions, we learn more about God, and we make our faith stronger. We make it easier for ourselves to obey God's commandments, and we make it easier for God to protect us from evil.

Out of long experience in battling evil, St. Paul gives us the following advice:

> Finally, be strong in the Lord and in the strength of his might. Put on the whole armor of God, that you may be able to stand against the wiles of the devil. —Ephesians 6:10-11

In this great hymn of our church, Martin Luther tells how Jesus protects us from evil:

A mighty fortress is our God,
A bulwark never failing;
Our helper he amid the flood
Of mortal ills prevailing:
For still our ancient foe
Doth seek to work us woe;
His craft and power are
*   great,*
And, armed with cruel hate,
On earth is not his equal.

Did we in our own strength confide
Our striving would be losing;
Were not the right Man on our
*   side,*
The Man of God's own choosing.
Dost ask who that may be?
Christ Jesus, it is he;
Lord Sabaoth his Name,
From age to age the same,
And he must win the battle.

—150 SBH, 262 LH

PRAYER

Dear Lord: Thank you for protecting me from evil. May I walk in your ways. Amen. The Lord's Prayer.

Sunday   *The First Article*

"All this he does out of fatherly . . . goodness . . ."

Many people who believe in God do not think of him as a Father. Rather, they think of him as some far-off, powerful force, which made the world and its people, but which has nothing more to do with them in a personal way. They do not think that God is interested in or cares about individual people, so they do not see any sense in praying to him.

But that is not the kind of a God the Bible tells us about. The heroes of the Old Testament knew God and his angel messengers very well and very personally and even talked and walked and wrestled with them. The name Israel means "I have wrestled with God." In the New Testament, Jesus always uses the word Father when he talks about God—his own Father and our Father.

God gives us his many blessings because he loves us like a father and because we are his children.

Jesus taught us to call God Father when we pray to him:

> Pray then like this:
> Our Father who art in heaven,
> Hallowed be thy name.
>
> —Matthew 6:9

In this hymn we sing about God as our Father and ourselves as his children:

> *Children of the heavenly Father*
> *Safely in his bosom gather;*
> *Nestling bird nor star in heaven*
> *Such a refuge e'er was given.*
>
> *God his own doth tend and nourish,*
> *In his holy courts they flourish.*
> *From all evil things he spares them,*
> *In his mighty arms he bears them.*
>
> —572 SBH

PRAYER

Dear heavenly Father: I thank you that I am your child and that you do all things for me out of fatherly goodness. Amen. The Lord's Prayer.

Monday

"All this he does out of . . . divine goodness . . ."

Even when we do what we call "good" deeds, there is almost always some false motive mixed in. When we give clothes or money or food to the poor or to Lutheran World Action, it is not always out of pure goodness. Sometimes we give because we are asked so often; sometimes we give because we do not want others to think we are cheapskates; sometimes we give because we are afraid of what God will do to us if we don't; sometimes we give things we don't want or need. These are certainly not purely good reasons.

But God gives his gifts to us out of divine goodness. One characteristic of divine goodness is that it is pure goodness, without any other motives mixed in. One proof that God gives out of pure goodness is that he gives his blessings of nature (the sun and rain, the soil, and the gift of life) to everyone, including both good and bad people. God does nothing because he wants a reward; he gives his gifts because he wants the best for us. That is divine, pure goodness, which only God can show.

Jesus does not want us to love only nice people, but those who need it most:

> But I say to you, Love your enemies and pray for those who persecute you, so that you may be sons of your Father who is in heaven; for he makes his sun rise on the evil and on the good, and sends rain on the just and on the unjust.
> —Matthew 5:44-45

Here is a hymn about the goodness of God:

> *The King of love my shepherd is,*
> *Whose goodness faileth never;*
> *I nothing lack if I am his,*
> *And he is mine forever.*

> *In death's dark vale I fear no ill*
> *With thee, dear Lord, beside me,*
> *Thy rod and staff my comfort still,*
> *Thy Cross before to guide me.*
> —530 SBH, 431 LH

PRAYER

Dear heavenly Father: I thank you that you do all things for me out of pure, divine goodness. Help me to show goodness to others. Amen. The Lord's Prayer.

93

Tuesday *The First Article*

"All this he does out of ... divine goodness ..."

We have said that God is a personal God, with whom the people of Old Testament times talked, and whose favorite name in the New Testament is Father. But we must not for a moment forget that God is not just a person who is human. God is super-human, or more-than-human. That is what the word "divine" means.

When we say that God does things for us "out of divine goodness," we mean that his goodness is above human goodness. For one thing, it is pure goodness, as we have already said. For another thing, God's goodness is dependable: it can always be counted on; it never fails. Humans are good one day and not so good the next. We may be good to our family in the morning and mean to them the same afternoon.

But God's goodness, because it is divine, because it is above our goodness, is always the same. The sun never fails, the seasons always come, new life is continually being born, and he is always ready to forgive us our sins when we are truly sorry for them.

The prophet Isaiah tells us that God's goodness is not the same as ours:

> For as the heavens are higher than the earth,
> so are my ways higher than your ways
> and my thoughts than your thoughts.
> —Isaiah 55:9

We sing about the dependable goodness of God in this hymn:

> *O Lord of heaven and earth and sea,*
> *To thee all praise and glory be;*
> *How shall we show our love to thee,*
> *Who givest all?*

> *The golden sunshine, vernal air,*
> *Sweet flowers and fruit thy love declare,*
> *When harvests ripen, thou art there,*
> *Who givest all.*
> —448 SBH, 443 LH

PRAYER

Dear heavenly Father: I thank you that your goodness and love never fail. Amen. The Lord's Prayer.

Wednesday   *The First Article*

"All this he does out of . . . goodness . . ."

Ideals are ideas that we have about how people and things ought to be, but never are. For instance, most young people do not think of George Washington or Abraham Lincoln as real human men at all, but rather as saints or supermen. But when we read the personal papers of Washington and Lincoln, we learn that, although they were great men, they were, after all, only men. Artists often paint people and places much lovelier than they really are, and writers also idealize people and places and events in history.

How does it happen that people can have such ideals of things? Where do the ideals come from? They come from God. It is from him that we get the idea of how people and things ought to be, even if they never are like that. It is from God that we get the ideal of goodness, of perfect goodness. It is because we know Jesus and his love for us that we know what true goodness is and that we can try to practice it in our lives.

This psalm thanks God for his goodness:

> O give thanks to the Lord, for he is good;
> for his steadfast love endures for ever!
> —Psalm 107:1

We praise the goodness of God in this hymn:

> *Praise ye the Father for his loving kindness;*
> *Tenderly cares he for his erring children;*
> *Praise him, ye angels, praise him in the heavens,*
> *Praise ye Jehovah.*

> *Praise ye the Saviour, great is his compassion;*
> *Graciously cares he for his chosen people;*
> *Young men and maidens, ye old men and children,*
> *Praise ye the Saviour.*
> —421 SBH

PRAYER

Dear heavenly Father: I thank you for the ideal of goodness which you have given me. Help me more and more to live up to it. Amen. The Lord's Prayer.

"All this he does out of . . . mercy . . ."

At the end of the pledge to our American flag, we say, "One nation, under God, indivisible, with liberty and justice for all." The aim of the United States is to build a world-order based on international law, or justice.

But justice is not enough to hold a society or a nation or a world together. There must be mercy too. The Hebrew society of the Old Testament, and even of Christ's time, was based on justice with very little mercy. If a man took another man's eye out in a fight, the law demanded that his own eye be put out. If a man knocked another man's teeth out, his own were knocked out. If a woman was unfaithful to her husband, the law said she was to be taken outside the city walls and stoned to death. If a man said anything against God, he was also put to death.

When Christ came he taught men that God was love, and that they should show mercy to one another because God was merciful to them. If God were only just, without being merciful, none of us would be alive, because we have all done wrong and deserve his punishment. But out of mercy he forgives us and gives us all the blessings we enjoy.

This psalm reminds us of the mercy of the Lord:

> The Lord is merciful and gracious,
> slow to anger and abounding in steadfast love.
> —Psalm 103:8

God's mercy is praised in this favorite hymn:

> *There's a wideness in God's mercy,*
> *Like the wideness of the sea;*
> *There's a kindness in his justice,*
> *Which is more than liberty.*
>
> *There is no place where earth's sorrows*
> *Are more felt than up in heaven;*
> *There is no place where earth's failings*
> *Have such kindly judgment given.*
> —493 SBH

PRAYER

Dear heavenly Father: I thank you that you do all things for me out of mercy. Help me to show mercy toward others. Amen. The Lord's Prayer.

Friday   *The First Article*

"... though I do not deserve it."

It is in our nature to want to make a "deal" or a bargain. We will sit with the neighbor's baby for so much an hour. We will wash the storm windows for Dad at so much a window. We will shovel sidewalks for such and such a price.

The devil often makes us big-headed enough to want to bargain with God too. We think to ourselves, "I'll try real hard to do all the things I'm supposed to do this week, including going to both Sunday school and church, and then God will have to give me what I pray for." Or we get the idea that by doing certain things we can earn our way into heaven, and that God will have to "let us in."

It is sin of the worst kind to think that we can win merits from God for anything we do, or that he does things for us because we deserve them. We do not deserve or merit anything from God. Our sins far outnumber our merits. He does things for us out of his goodness and mercy, because he loves us. Whatever we do for him should be out of thankfulness for all he has done for us, not in order to bargain with him.

How we ought to feel toward God is stated in this psalm:

> What shall I render to the Lord
> for all his bounty to me?
>
> —Psalm 116:12

This hymn tells of the things God does for us without our deserving them:

> *Great God, we sing that mighty hand*
> *By which supported still we stand;*
> *The opening year thy mercy shows,*
> *Let mercy crown it till it close.*
>
> *By day, by night, at home, abroad,*
> *Still are we guarded by our God,*
> *By his incessant bounty fed,*
> *By his unerring counsel led.*
>
> —533 SBH, 119 LH

PRAYER

Dear heavenly Father: I thank you that you do all things for me without any merit on my part. Help me to love others as you have loved me. Amen. The Lord's Prayer.

Saturday   *The First Article*

"Therefore I surely ought to thank and praise, serve and obey him."

What would you think of someone who received an expensive gift and then said, "Thanks, but I feel I have it coming. I'm worthy of it"? You'd say he was the most conceited person you had ever heard of, and he shouldn't get the gift.

It is even more ridiculous and conceited for us to think that we have God's blessings coming and are worthy of them. What could we possibly do to deserve his gift of life, all the joys and blessings of home and family, the opportunities of the future?

The most we can do is accept all of these with great love and thankfulness to our heavenly Father and try to live a life pleasing to him.

This famous Bible passage reminds us of God's blessings truly given:

> The eyes of all look to thee,
>   and thou givest them their food in due season.
> Thou openest thy hand,
>   thou satisfiest the desire of every living thing.
> —Psalm 145:15-16

Here is another famous hymn that praises God for his goodness and mercy:

> *Praise to the Lord, who o'er all things so wondrously reigneth,*
> *Shelters thee under his wings, yea, so gently sustaineth:*
>   *Hast thou not seen?*
>   *All that is needful hath been*
> *Granted in what he ordaineth.*
>
> *Praise to the Lord, who doth prosper thy work and defend thee;*
> *Surely his goodness and mercy here daily attend thee.*
>   *Ponder anew*
>   *What the Almighty can do,*
> *If with his love he befriend thee!*
>
> —408 SBH, 39 LH

PRAYER

Dear heavenly Father: I thank you that you do all things for me without any worthiness on my part. Help me to be more obedient to your commands and to love you more. Amen. The Lord's Prayer.

Sunday   *The First Article*

"Therefore I surely ought . . ."

So far in this explanation of the first article of the Creed, we have learned all the things that God, the creator, has given to us or made possible for us to get for ourselves. That puts us in debt to God; it makes us "owe" him.

If some friend of ours does us a big favor, we feel that we must do something in return, not necessarily to pay the favor back, but to show our gratitude. How much more we ought to feel that way toward God, our heavenly Father, who not only has given us everything we have, but who has even created us!

No matter what we do for him, we can never actually pay him back for all he has done for us; but we should feel in debt to him. If we don't feel that way, we had better check up on our faith. Something very important is lacking!

In this psalm we are told not to forget God's goodness to us:

> Bless the Lord, O my soul;
> and all that is within me, bless his holy name!
> Bless the Lord, O my soul,
> and forget not all his benefits.
>
> —Psalm 103:1-2

The words of this hymn tell why we should feel indebted to God:

> *Thy bountiful care what tongue can recite?*
> *It breathes in the air, it shines in the light;*
> *It streams from the hills, it descends to the plain,*
> *And sweetly distils in the dew and the rain.*
>
> *Frail children of dust, and feeble as frail,*
> *In thee do we trust, nor find thee to fail;*
> *Thy mercies how tender, how firm to the end,*
> *Our Maker, Defender, Redeemer, and Friend.*
>
> —163 SBH, 17 LH

PRAYER

Dear heavenly Father: May I always feel that I ought to live my life to your honor and glory. Amen. The Lord's Prayer.

Monday   *The First Article*

"... I surely ought to thank ... him."

We often show the least gratitude to those who do the most for us. Many times we thank people for small favors that they do for us, but we hardly ever express our gratitude to our parents, who certainly do more for us than anyone else in the world. Probably it is because we are so used to accepting all the things Mother and Dad do for us and give us that we don't stop to think that they have any thanks coming.

It is much the same way with God. We are so used to the sun's shining and the rain's falling, so used to seeing the fields full of grain and gardens full of flowers, so used to being happy and healthy and having family and friends that we forget that it is God who has given us all these blessings and therefore we ought to thank him. If we forget too long, perhaps one day God will stop sending us some of these blessings. Let us remember to thank him before it is too late.

The psalm writer remembers to give thanks to God:

> Then we thy people, the flock of thy pasture,
> will give thanks to thee for ever;
> from generation to generation we will
> recount thy praise.
> —Psalm 79:13

This hymn praises God as the giver of all blessings:

> *When all thy mercies, O my God,*
> *My rising soul surveys,*
> *Transported with the view,*
> *I'm lost in wonder, love, and praise!*
>
> *Ten thousand thousand precious gifts*
> *My daily thanks employ;*
> *Nor is the least a cheerful heart*
> *That tastes those gifts with joy.*
> —440 SBH, 31 LH

PRAYER

Dear heavenly Father: May I always remember to be thankful to you for all my blessings. Amen. The Lord's Prayer.

Tuesday   *The First Article*

". . . I surely ought to . . . praise . . . him."

The dictionary says that to praise means "to express approval or admiration of; to magnify, to glorify." We praise generals who win wars, actors and musicians who give outstanding performances, athletes who win contests, and politicians who win elections. We show our approval and admiration for such people because they have done great things.

How much more we ought to praise God, who has done far greater things than any human being, who has created us and the world we live in!

That is one good reason for going to church and Sunday school. There we join with other Christians in worshiping and praising God.

In the Psalms we have some of our greatest hymns of praise to God:

> Praise the Lord!
> Praise God in his sanctuary;
>   praise him in his mighty firmament!
> Praise him for his mighty deeds;
>   praise him according to his exceeding greatness!
> —Psalm 150:1-2

Here is one of many hymns of praise in our hymnal:

Let the whole creation cry,
'Glory to the Lord on high!'
Heaven and earth awake and sing,
'God is good and therefore King!'
Praise him, all ye hosts above,
Ever bright and fair in love;
Sun and moon, uplift your voice,
Night and stars, in God rejoice!

Men and women, young and old,
Raise the anthem manifold,
And let children's happy hearts
In this worship bear their parts;
From the north to southern pole
Let the mighty chorus roll:
'Holy, holy, holy One,
Glory be to God alone!'
—414 SBH

PRAYER

Dear heavenly Father: Help me to be in my place in church and Sunday school to praise you for all the wonderful things you have done. Amen. The Lord's Prayer.

Wednesday   *The First Article*

". . . I surely ought to . . . serve . . . him."

In one of our past devotions we said that society couldn't go on unless people served or did their part. The older we become, the more responsibility society puts on us, and the more we are expected to serve. Every once in a while we read or hear about some man or woman who carries an unusual amount of responsibility. He or she may be president of a company, a director on several boards, a member of a half dozen lodges and clubs, or a member of the state legislature.

Perhaps you would like to grow up to be that kind of person. But we have to remember that as Christians we are really members of two societies: one on earth and one in heaven. One is a worldly society and the other is a spiritual society which we call the kingdom of God. That kingdom needs servants too—people who will take on a great deal of responsibility in the church, which is the organization trying to do the work of God's kingdom in this world. A Christian ought to serve God in some way.

Joshua gives his people advice which is good for us too:

> Take good care to observe the commandment and the law which Moses the servant of the Lord commanded you, to love the Lord your God, and to walk in all his ways, and to keep his commandments, and to cleave to him, and to serve him with all your heart and with all your soul.
>
> —Joshua 22:5

Here is a hymn that asks for servants in God's church:

> *Rise up, O men of God!*
> *Have done with lesser things;*
> *Give heart and soul and mind and strength*
> *To serve the King of kings.*
>
> *Rise up, O men of God!*
> *The Church for you doth wait,*
> *Her strength unequal to her task;*
> *Rise up and make her great!*
>
> —541 SBH

PRAYER

Dear heavenly Father: Help me to do my duty toward you by serving you in every way I possibly can, especially through your church. Amen. The Lord's Prayer.

Thursday   *The First Article*

"... I surely ought to ... serve ... him."

One way to serve God is with our talents. There has never been so much talent in the world as there is today. The radio and TV and the movies must have great numbers of talented people to keep going, and all our thousands of schools and colleges and universities help to develop talent in all fields, from medicine and science to art and music. You can have the finest talent brought right into your own living room through radio and television. Each year tens of thousands of young people begin careers as artists, musicians, actors, or writers.

The world is getting more talent than it can use, but how much is God getting? His church has always suffered from not having talent enough. The Protestant Church in America is short more than 20,000 ministers. All of our churches need people who can do office work, who can sing, who can teach, who can lead young people's groups. Can you do any of these things? Have you thought about using your talents to serve the church, either full or part time? After all, it is God who gave you your talents when you were born. Therefore you ought to use them in his service.

Jesus himself calls us to serve him:

> If any one serves me, he must follow me; and where I am, there shall my servant be also; if any one serves me, the Father will honor him.
>
> —John 12:26

This hymn tells us why we ought to serve God:

Thy life was given for me,
  Thy blood, O Lord, was shed
That I might ransomed be,
  And quickened from the dead.
Thy life was given for me,
What have I given for thee?

O let my life be given,
  My years for thee be spent;
World-fetters all be riven,
  And joy with suffering blent.
Thou gav'st thyself for me,
I give myself to thee.
  —513 SBH

PRAYER

Dear heavenly Father: Help me to do my duty toward you by serving you with my talents and abilities. Amen. The Lord's Prayer.

Friday   *The First Article*

"... I surely ought to ... serve ... him."

Another way of serving God is to give money for his use. If you have been thinking that when the pastor talks about giving money to the church he is talking to the grownups only, you have certainly been wrong. He has been talking to every one who has any money to spend.

Just how much money do you as a young person spend for yourself—for the things you need and want? You spend money at the show, at the drugstore, at the department store. You spend money on your bikes, on your skates, and on clothes. You do spend money.

Now the question is, "Am I giving any of it to God for his work?" No matter how small an amount of money you do have each week or month, you can give some of it—if it is only a single penny—to God and his church. That will show that you appreciate all that he has done for you, and it will get you into the habit of giving. Then when you are older and do have more money, you will be used to giving a part of it to God. If you do that, God has promised that he will bless you much more than if you keep all your money for yourself.

Jesus tells us that by giving we also receive:

> Give, and it will be given to you; good measure, pressed down, shaken together, running over, will be put into your lap. For the measure you give will be the measure you get back.
>
> —Luke 6:38

We often use this hymn to bless the offering received in church:

> *We give thee but thine own,*
> *Whate'er the gift may be;*
> *All that we have is thine alone,*
> *A trust, O Lord, from thee.*
>
> *May we thy bounties thus*
> *As stewards true receive,*
> *And gladly, as thou blessest us,*
> *To thee our first-fruits give.*
>
> —544 SBH, 441 LH

PRAYER

Dear heavenly Father: Help me to serve you by setting aside a certain part of my money for the work of your kingdom. Amen. The Lord's Prayer.

"... I surely ought to ... obey him."

We have talked quite a bit in these devotions about obeying God. But there is still more we can say about it because it is so important. Suppose you were in the middle of a jungle, surrounded by enemies who wanted to kill you, and you did not know any way out. Then suddenly a man came up to you and said, "I know the way out of here, and I will lead you to safety if you will follow me and do as I say." You would jump at the chance, wouldn't you? You would obey this man because he knows the way out and you do not. Your life is in his hands.

Well, God comes to us and wants to lead us to heaven. He knows we don't know the way by ourselves; we would get lost a thousand times a day on our own; and our enemy, the devil, would soon have us. So God asks us to follow him and do as he tells us. If we accept him as our leader, then we are in duty bound to obey him as we would any other leader we choose. If we do not obey him, he cannot lead us. And if he cannot lead us, we are lost.

> Yea, thou art my rock and my fortress;
>   for thy name's sake lead me and guide me,
> take me out of the net which is hidden for me,
>   for thou art my refuge.
>
> —Psalm 31:3-4

One of the great hymns of our church asks God to be our guide:

> Guide me, O thou great Jehovah,
>   Pilgrim through this barren land;
> I am weak, but thou art mighty,
>   Hold me with thy powerful hand;
>   Bread of heaven,
>   Feed me till I want no more.
>
> —520 SBH, 54 LH

PRAYER

Dear heavenly Father: Help me to do my duty toward you by studying and learning your commandments and obeying them in my daily life. Amen. The Lord's Prayer.

"I believe that Jesus Christ . . ."

The name Jesus is really from the Greek form of the well-known Hebrew name Jeshua or Joshua, which means *"God Is Salvation."* You remember that it was Joshua, the great soldier, whom God chose to lead the Hebrew people into the Promised Land of Canaan, after Moses died. Joshua, or Jesus, was a common, well-loved name among the Hebrews, and when parents gave it to their children it meant they had faith in God as the Savior of his people.

The name Christ is from the Greek form of the Hebrew Mashiah, or Messiah as we spell it. The Messiah was the Savior whom the prophets had said God would send to save his people from all their troubles.

So we see that Jesus Christ means man's Savior, sent from God. We know that is exactly who Jesus was; he was God himself, come down to earth to save men from their sins.

These words of the angel to Joseph tell us that the name Jesus means Savior:

> She will bear a son, and you shall call his name Jesus, for
> he will save his people from their sins.
> —Matthew 1:21

Here is a hymn about the name of Jesus:

> *How sweet the Name of Jesus sounds*
> *In a believer's ear!*
> *It soothes his sorrows, heals his wounds,*
> *And drives away his fear.*
>
> *It makes the wounded spirit whole,*
> *And calms the troubled breast;*
> *'Tis manna to the hungry soul,*
> *And to the weary rest.*
>
> *Dear Name! the rock on which I build,*
> *My shield and hiding-place;*
> *My never-failing treasury filled*
> *With boundless stores of grace.*
> —406 SBH, 364 LH

PRAYER

Dear Lord Jesus: I thank you that you are my Savior. Help me to put my trust in you. Amen. The Lord's Prayer.

"I believe that Jesus Christ—true God . . ."

When we say that we believe Jesus Christ is "true" God, we mean that we believe he is really God. Many people, even some who claim to be Christians, do not believe that Christ is really God. Some believe that he was a great teacher, perhaps the greatest that ever lived. But they do not believe he is God. Others believe he was the greatest prophet of all time, but that does not make him God. Still others believe that Jesus Christ was the kindest and purest man that ever lived. But they do not believe he is God.

Christians must believe that Christ is God or they are not Christians because to be a Christian means to believe that Christ saves us from sin and eternal death, and no mere man—no human being—could do that for us.

We say in our Creed that Jesus is the "only Son" of God. We say that Jesus is God's Son because we are only human and we have to think and talk in human terms. We can understand the Jesus who was on earth only in that way. To the Jews of Jesus' day the Son of God was equal to, or the same as, God. Jesus himself said, "He who has seen me has seen the Father." Jesus Christ is God, the real God, the true God, the one who alone can save us.

Jesus tells his disciples that he is God:

> If you had known me, you would have known my Father also; henceforth you know him and have seen him.
>
> —John 14:7

We call Jesus God in this hymn:

> *Jesus, my Lord, my God, my all,*
> *Hear me, blest Saviour, when I call;*
> *Hear me, and from thy dwelling place*
> *Pour down the riches of thy grace.*
> *Jesus, my Lord, I thee adore,*
> *O make me love thee more and more.*
>
> —504 SBH

PRAYER

Dear Lord Jesus: I am thankful that because of you I can know who God truly is. Amen. The Lord's Prayer.

Tuesday   *The Second Article*

"... Son of the Father ..."

A favorite question that Sunday school children ask is: "If Jesus is God, then who was he praying to when he was on earth?" Since we are only human beings, and not God, there are some things we will never be able to understand, at least in this life. One such thing is how God can be everywhere at once: in heaven and on earth too.

In order to tell us about such a God in a way we can understand, the New Testament tells us about the Father and the Son: how the Father sent his Son into the world to die for our sins and how he raised him up from the dead to win everlasting life for us. But the Father and the Son are really the same God. Jesus is God.

According to Jesus' own words he is God:

I and the Father are one.

—John 10:30

We praise Jesus in this hymn as both Son of God and God:

Crown Him the Son of God
Before the worlds began;
And ye who tread where He hath trod,
Crown Him the Son of Man,
Who ev'ry grief hath known
That wrings the human breast,
And takes and bears them for His own
That all in Him may rest.

Crown Him the Lord of heaven,
Enthroned in worlds above,
Crown Him the King to Whom is given
The wondrous name of Love.
Crown Him with many crowns
As thrones before Him fall,
Crown Him, ye kings, with many crowns,
For He is King of all.

—134 CSB

PRAYER

Dear Lord Jesus: May I always worship you as my true Lord and Savior. Amen. The Lord's Prayer.

Wednesday   *The Second Article*

"... Son of the Father from eternity ..."

The Bible teaches us not only that Christ was Son of God but that he was so from eternity, or from the beginning of time. We human beings have a very small idea of time. We think of people who live 80 years as being very old. We think that it was a long, long time ago that Columbus discovered America or that Christ was born in Bethlehem. We call the study of how men lived two and three thousand years ago "ancient history." That is the way we see it.

But compared to the age of our earth and other planets and stars of our universe—hundreds of thousands or perhaps even millions of years—our idea of a long time is only a short second. The length of our life, compared to the length of time the world has been here would be like one minute compared to a year.

God is the only one who sees time as it really is. As the Bible says, a thousand years to him is like a day. The first words of the Bible are: "In the beginning God created the heavens and the earth." That means that he existed before anything that he made and before time, as we know it, ever began. And right from that "beginning" or from "eternity," the New Testament tells us, Christ was with God. Christ is not only one with God now, but he was always—from eternity—one with God.

The New Testament calls Jesus "the Word" and says he was always with God:

> In the beginning was the Word, and the Word was with God, and the Word was God. He was in the beginning with God; all things were made through him, and without him was not anything made that was made.
>
> —John 1:1-3

In this hymn we say that God and Christ are eternal:

> *Eternal are thy mercies, Lord,*
> *Eternal truth attends thy word;*
> *Thy praise shall sound from shore to shore,*
> *Till suns shall rise and set no more.*
> —429 SBH, 15 LH

PRAYER

Dear Lord Jesus: I am thankful that you will be my God forever and ever. Amen. The Lord's Prayer.

109

Thursday   *The Second Article*

"... and true man ..."

We have been saying that Jesus Christ is truly God, really God. Now we are saying that he was also truly man. How is that possible? Why should our Lord be both God and man?

First of all, we must remember that all things are possible for God, who created the heavens and the earth and all the life in them, including people. We must have faith enough in God's almighty power to believe that he could become a person himself if he thought it was necessary. And why was it necessary? It was necessary in order that God might lead people back to himself in a way they could understand. What better way could God make us understand than to become a person himself, who by his perfect life and speech would show people what God was like? By becoming a true man himself, and by going through sorrows and temptations and death like other people, God showed us that he is truly our Lord, who understands our troubles and who loved us enough to become one of us.

St. Paul tells us about Christ's becoming true man:

> ... who, though he was in the form of God, did not count equality with God a thing to be grasped, but emptied himself, taking the form of a servant, being born in the likeness of men. And being found in human form he humbled himself and became obedient unto death, even death on a cross.
> —Philippians 2:6-8

This Lenten hymn tells about Christ's becoming human for our sakes:

> *O Christ, our King, Creator, Lord,*
> *Saviour of all who trust thy word,*
> *To them who seek thee ever near,*
> *Now to our praises bend thine ear.*
>
> *Now in the Father's glory high,*
> *Great Conqueror, never more to die,*
> *Us by thy mighty power defend,*
> *And reign through ages without end.*

> —62 SBH

PRAYER

Dear Lord Jesus: I am thankful that you do understand and sympathize with troubles and temptations. Amen. The Lord's Prayer.

110

Friday   *The Second Article*

"... born of the Virgin Mary ..."

Hundreds of years before the birth of Christ the prophet Isaiah, speaking the Word of God, said that a virgin would have a son who would be a leader of his people. The prophet Micah said that this great leader, or Messiah, would be born in Bethlehem. It was also prophesied that the Messiah or Savior would come from the family of David, Israel's greatest king.

Now when Jesus was born to Mary and Joseph, all these prophecies came true, but in a way no human being could have guessed. Mary was a young woman of the town of Nazareth, and she and Joseph were married there. The only reason Jesus was born in Bethlehem instead of Nazareth was that the Roman emperor had ordered that everyone must go to the town or city of his ancestors to be taxed. Since Joseph and Mary were both from the family of David, and David's city was Bethlehem, Joseph and Mary had to go there to register, and on the very evening they arrived, Mary's son was born in the stable of the town's only inn. Instead of God's coming to earth as a baby born to wealthy and famous parents in a palace in some big city, he chose to be born of poor, unknown people, in a stable in a little country town.

Isaiah prophesied concerning the birth of Jesus:

> For to us a child is born, to us a son is given; and the government will be upon his shoulder, and his name will be called Wonderful Counselor, Mighty God, Everlasting Father, Prince of Peace.
>
> —Isaiah 9:6

We sing of Jesus' birth in this Christmas hymn:

> *All praise to thee, Eternal Lord,*
> *Clothed in a garb of flesh and blood;*
> *Choosing a manger for thy throne,*
> *While worlds on worlds are thine alone.*
>
> —21 SBH, 80 LH

PRAYER

Dear Lord Jesus: Help me to be humble when I remember your birth in the stable at Bethlehem. Amen. The Lord's Prayer.

"I believe that Jesus Christ . . . is my Lord."

In the olden days a knight was the lord of his castle and the land around it. That meant that he was the master of all the people who lived and worked in the buildings and on the land. His word was law, and everyone obeyed him without question. But the lord took care of the people too. He saw to it that they had food and clothing; he settled their quarrels; he protected them in time of danger. They looked to him as their protector and provider.

Jesus is our Lord, our Master, our Protector, and our Provider. It is out of love for us that he became our Lord; that he came to earth to live among us and to show us the way to God; that he took upon himself our sin in order that we might not be guilty before God; that he conquered sin and the devil and even death itself so that we might believe in him and have everlasting life. No other lord has ever done such things for his people and no other lord ever will. Jesus Christ is the Lord of all lords.

The New Testament promises that the time is coming when every person and every thing will call Jesus Lord:

> . . . that at the name of Jesus every knee should bow, in heaven and on earth and under the earth, and every tongue confess that Jesus Christ is Lord, to the glory of God the Father.
>
> —Philippians 2:10-11

This hymn praises Christ as Lord:

> *The head that once was crowned with thorns*
> *Is crowned with glory now;*
> *A royal diadem adorns*
> *The mighty Victor's brow.*
>
> *The highest place that heaven affords*
> *Is his, is his by right,*
> *The King of kings, and Lord of lords,*
> *And heaven's eternal Light.*
>
> —439 SBH, 219 LH

PRAYER

Dear Lord Jesus: I am thankful that you are my Lord. Help me to be your worthy servant. Amen. The Lord's Prayer.

112

Sunday   *The Second Article*

"He has redeemed me ..."

When a person redeems something, he buys it back again after it has been lost to him. Parents of a child who has been kidnaped try to redeem their child, or get him back, by paying a ransom.

We call Christ our Redeemer because he came to earth in human form to bring us back to God, and he gave his own life on the cross as the ransom. Or, to put it another way, when you redeem something you save it. We call Christ our Redeemer because he came to save us.

St. Paul spoke of Jesus as Savior and Redeemer:

> ... awaiting our blessed hope, the appearing of the glory of our great God and Savior Jesus Christ, who gave himself for us to redeem us from all iniquity and to purify for himself a people of his own who are zealous for good deeds.
> —Titus 2:13-14

A favorite hymn of the Christian church sings of Jesus as Redeemer:

> *I know that my Redeemer lives:*
> *What joy the blest assurance gives!*
> *He lives, he lives who once was dead;*
> *He lives, my everlasting head!*
>
> *He lives, all glory to his Name;*
> *He lives, my Saviour, still the same;*
> *What joy the blest assurance gives:*
> *I know that my Redeemer lives!*
> —387 SBH, 200 LH

PRAYER

Dear Lord Jesus: May I always be grateful to you for giving your life to redeem me. Amen. The Lord's Prayer.

"He has redeemed me . . ."

Many people ask the question, "Why do we need a Redeemer or Savior? Aren't we all right without one?" There are many ways to answer that question. The easiest way to answer it is to take a look at ourselves. If we are honest, we will admit that we do, say, and think many things that we know are wrong. But if we know they are wrong, why do we keep on doing and saying and thinking such things? We keep on because the devil has power over us. He makes us want to disobey God, and he makes doing what is right seem very hard and often unpleasant.

Ever since Adam and Eve listened to the devil, we human beings have been under the power of evil, and only Christ can break this power and save us.

Even such a great man as the Apostle Paul said that he was under the power of evil:

> Now if I do what I do not want, it is no longer I that do it, but sin which dwells within me. So I find it to be a law that when I want to do right, evil lies close at hand.
>
> —Romans 7:20-21

Luther tells how only Christ can defeat the devil:

> *Did we in our own strength confide*
> *Our striving would be losing;*
> *Were not the right Man on our side,*
> *The Man of God's own choosing.*
> *Dost ask who that may be?*
> *Christ Jesus, it is he;*
> *Lord Sabaoth his Name,*
> *From age to age the same,*
> *And he must win the battle.*
>
> —150 SBH, 262 LH

PRAYER

Dear Lord Jesus: I am grateful that you have saved me from my sins. Help me to grow spiritually stronger every day. Amen. The Lord's Prayer.

Tuesday   *The Second Article*

"... a lost ... person ..."

Have you ever been lost? It is a frightening feeling. Men have been lost for days in the woods and have been found only a few feet from a road they did not know was there. Experienced woodsmen carry a compass, so that if they should become confused in country they do not know, they will be able to tell where north is and so find the way.

After the first people God created disobeyed him, they and their children and all the generations that came after them listened to the devil more and more until they no longer knew God's way of living. They became lost, and instead of following the way of peace and goodness and love, they took the way of hatred and evil and war.

Christ is our compass that always points to God. If we follow him, we will get back on the right road. Without him we are as lost as if we were in a strange woods without a compass.

Jesus speaks of himself as the Savior of those who are lost:

> For the Son of man came to seek and to save the lost.
> —Luke 19:10

We ask Jesus in this hymn to be our Guide through life and death:

> *Jesus, Saviour, pilot me*
> *Over life's tempestuous sea;*
> *Unknown waves before me roll,*
> *Hiding rock and treacherous shoal;*
> *Chart and compass come from thee,*
> *Jesus, Saviour, pilot me.*
>
> *When at last I near the shore,*
> *And the fearful breakers roar*
> *'Twixt me and the peaceful rest,*
> *Then, while leaning on my breast,*
> *May I hear thee say to me,*
> *'Fear not, I will pilot thee.'*
> —531 SBH, 649 LH

PRAYER

Dear Lord Jesus: I pray that you will lead and guide and keep me in the right way all my life. Amen. The Lord's Prayer.

". . . a condemned person . . ."

To be condemned means to be pronounced guilty. When we break the law (going through a stop sign, for instance) and we are caught, we are pronounced guilty and punished. We expect to be punished when we break the law. We would not think very much of any judge who would not condemn and punish those who violate the law. He would be dishonest.

When we disobey God, we break the law too—the moral law—the rules God has laid down to guide our lives. If God is an honest God, he must condemn us if we break his law. It would be dishonest for God to look the other way and act as though we had not done anything wrong. We do break God's law, not only once, but many, many times, all our lives. Therefore God's punishment would have to be so great we could not live under it. It would mean death for all time for us.

But God is not only just; he is also merciful and loving. And so he sent his only Son to save us who are condemned, if we will believe in him and trust in him.

The Bible tells us that Jesus saves us from condemnation:

> There is therefore now no condemnation for those who are in Christ Jesus. For the law of the Spirit of life in Christ Jesus has set me free from the law of sin and death.
> —Romans 8:1-2

We sing in this hymn about how we depend on Jesus to save us from our sins:

> *My hope is built on nothing less*
> *Than Jesus' Blood and righteousness;*
> *No merit of my own I claim,*
> *But wholly lean on Jesus' Name.*
> *On Christ, the solid rock, I stand;*
> *All other ground is sinking sand.*
>
> *His oath, his covenant, his Blood,*
> *Support me in the whelming flood;*
> *When all around my soul gives way,*
> *He then is all my hope and stay.*
> *On Christ, the solid rock I stand;*
> *All other ground is sinking sand.*
> —385 SBH, 370 LH

PRAYER

Dear Lord Jesus: I thank you for saving me from my sins. Amen. The Lord's Prayer.

Thursday   *The Second Article*

". . . saved me at great cost from sin . . ."

Without Christ to help us fight against evil, one sin leads to another until our thoughts and words and actions get out of our control altogether. There are examples all around us of people who are losing or have lost the battle against the temptations to sin. Alcohol has complete power over many people. Others have become slaves to smoking until their health has been ruined. Some cannot speak a single sentence without cursing. The number of crimes of all kinds committed by young people is increasing greatly every year. The more we sin, the harder it becomes not to sin; and finally we are hardly able to tell right from wrong.

In his life and death here on earth Jesus overcame the power of sin and set us an example of a perfect life. If we believe in him, he will secure and deliver us from the power of sin by sending his Holy Spirit to help us fight against it.

St. Paul tells about the difference Christ's Spirit makes in a person's life:

> But the fruit of the Spirit is love, joy, peace, patience, kindness, goodness, faithfulness, gentleness, self-control; against such there is no law. And those who belong to Christ Jesus have crucified the flesh with its passions and desires.
> —Galatians 5:22-24

We share our thankfulness to Christ in this hymn for delivering us from our sins:

> *How blessed from the bonds of sin*
> *And earthly fetters free,*
> *In singleness of heart and aim*
> *Thy servant, Lord, to be!*
> *The hardest toil to undertake*
> *With joy at thy command,*
> *The meanest office to receive*
> *With meekness at thy hand!*

> —60 SBH, 258 CSB

PRAYER

Dear Lord Jesus: Be with me always and give me the strength to do your will. Amen. The Lord's Prayer.

117

"... saved me at great cost from ... death ..."

When God created the first people, he wanted them to live forever. But because they disobeyed God, he could not let them live forever. When we study the Old Testament we see that as men sinned more and more, their lives became shorter and shorter. So one of the penalties we pay for sin is death. But Jesus showed us that death does not have to be forever. He conquered death by rising again on the third day after he was crucified. Christ not only conquered sin by living a perfect life, but he conquered death, which is the result of sin, by his resurrection on Easter morning. The promise of Easter is the most wonderful part of our Christian faith. Christ has promised that all those who believe in him as their Savior will also be raised from the dead when he comes again. Christ saved us at great cost from both sin and death.

Jesus assures a woman that those who believe in him will live forever:

> Jesus said to her, "Your brother will rise again." Martha said to him, "I know that he will rise again in the resurrection at the last day." Jesus said to her, "I am the resurrection and the life; he who believes in me, though he die, yet shall he live."
>
> —John 11:23-25

In this famous Easter hymn we sing about our victory in Christ over death:

> *Christ is risen! henceforth never*
> *Death or hell shall us enthrall;*
> *Be we Christ's, in Him for ever*
> *We have triumphed over all;*
> *All the doubting and dejection*
> *Of our trembling hearts have ceased;*
> *'Tis His day of Resurrection!*
> *Let us rise and keep the Feast.*
>
> —117 CSB

PRAYER

Dear Lord Jesus: May I share in your victory over death by being a true follower of yours in my daily life. Amen. The Lord's Prayer.

         The Second Article

". . . saved me at great cost from . . . the power of the devil."

When we see or hear the word devil, most of us think of a red, man-like creature, with horns and a tail, holding a pitchfork in his hand. We get those ideas from the pictures we have seen. If the devil were as funny as that, and we could actually see him, we would not have very much to worry about. But the devil is not a human being. He is a spiritual, super-human power who is against God and who is always trying to get as many human beings as he can to turn against God. By ourselves we are no match for him—he soon overpowers us or tricks us into his plans without our even knowing it. To fight this super-human power, we need another super-human power; we need Christ, who alone can conquer the devil and make us safe from his power.

St. Paul tells us that the devil is more than a human enemy:

> For we are not contending against flesh and blood, but against the principalities, against the powers, against the world rulers of this present darkness, against the spiritual hosts of wickedness in the heavenly places. Therefore take the whole armor of God, that you may be able to withstand in the evil day, and having done all, to stand.
>
> —Ephesians 6:12-13

The great founder of our church, Martin Luther, also knew how powerful the devil was and how we need Christ on our side against him:

> *A mighty Fortress is our God,*
> *A trusty Shield and Weapon;*
> *He helps us free from ev'ry need*
> *That hath us now o'ertaken.*
> *The old bitter foe*
> *Means us deadly woe;*
> *Deep guile and great might*
> *Are his dread arms in fight;*
> *On earth is not his equal.*
>
> —262 LH, 195 CSB

PRAYER

Dear Lord Jesus: Stand by me and help me to fight the devil when he tries to tempt me. Amen. The Lord's Prayer.

"... not with silver and gold ..."

To give money is often an easy way out. It is easier to give money to a political campaign than to go from house to house to get votes for your candidate or make speeches for him. It is easier to give money to Lutheran Welfare or Lutheran World Action than actually to take a poor person into your home and take care of him. It is easier to put your envelope in the offering plate on Sunday than to do any real work for the church. Oftentimes giving money is a cover-up for not giving ourselves—our time and energy. But our Lord loved us too much to redeem us, or get us back, with "silver and gold." He could have had all the silver and gold in the world if he had wanted it, but that would have been the easy way out, and the easy way is almost never the best way. The price to get us back to God was more than money could pay. The price had to be himself, and he loved us so much that he gave himself as the Lamb to be slain.

St. Paul felt he owed his life to Christ:

> I have been crucified with Christ; it is no longer I who live, but Christ who lives in me; and the life I now live in the flesh I live by faith in the Son of God, who loved me and gave himself for me.
>
> —Galatians 2:20

Our Lenten hymns remind us that Christ gave himself for us:

> *Wide open are thy hands,*
> *Paying with more than gold*
> *The aweful debt of guilty men,*
> *Forever and of old.*
> *Ah, let me grasp those hands,*
> *That we may never part,*
> *And let the power of their blood*
> *Sustain my fainting heart.*
>
> —66 SBH

PRAYER

Dear Christ, my Savior: I thank you that you gave yourself for me. Amen. The Lord's Prayer.

Monday   *The Second Article*

". . . but with his holy . . . blood . . ."

The custom of sacrificing a living thing to a god is as old as the history of man. The Bible tells us that Cain and Abel, the first children of the first human beings, offered sacrifices to God, and that Abel sacrificed the "firstlings of his flock." Living sacrifice has not only been carried on all through Jewish history, but the pagans also offered sacrifices to their gods. Sometimes they killed human beings on their altars. The blood from the sacrificed animal or person was supposed to purify those on whom it was sprinkled. In the 12th chapter of the Book of Exodus we read that the blood of the passover lamb on the doors of the houses saved the people of Israel from the plague that God sent against Egypt. So when Christ gave himself on the cross and shed his blood for us, he was offering himself as the lamb to be sacrificed, and giving his own blood to purify and save us. But his blood was holy, as no other blood could be, for he was the Son of God. His blood saves us as the blood of no sheep or goat or ox or human being can ever save us.

St. Paul talks about this in the following verses:

> For if the sprinkling of defiled persons with the blood of goats and bulls and with the ashes of a heifer sanctifies for the purification of the flesh, how much more shall the blood of Christ, who through the eternal Spirit offered himself without blemish to God, purify your conscience from dead works to serve the living God.
>
> —Hebrews 9:13-14

Here is a beautiful children's hymn about Christ's death:

> *He died that we might be forgiven,*
> *He died to make us good;*
> *That we might go at last to heaven,*
> *Saved by his precious Blood.*
>
> —77 SBH

PRAYER

Dear Christ, my Savior: May I give myself for you as you have given yourself for me. Amen. The Lord's Prayer.

"... but with his ... precious blood ..."

If someone is precious to us it means that we value and love him very much. When a new baby is born into a family, it becomes the most precious, the most loved member of that family. When two people are in love, they are precious to each other. Our parents are precious to us because of all the love and care and protection they give us. Most of us do not realize how precious others are until death takes them away; and then, all too late, we suddenly feel lost and alone, and we know how much their love meant to us. If the lives of other people can mean so much to us, how precious the life of our Lord ought to be! Think of what a terrible loss it was to the disciples when Jesus was crucified. He had been their friend and teacher and master. Think of what it meant to God to allow his only Son to give his life on the cross. We are saved by the most precious life and blood the world has ever known.

St. Peter speaks of the blood of Christ as precious:

> You know that you were ransomed from the futile ways inherited from your fathers, not with perishable things such as silver or gold, but with the precious blood of Christ, like that of a lamb without blemish or spot.
>
> —1 Peter 1:18-19

We remember Jesus' sacrifice for us in this Lenten hymn:

> *Glory be to Jesus,*
> *Who, in bitter pains,*
> *Poured for me the lifeblood*
> *From his sacred veins!*
>
> *Lift we then our voices,*
> *Swell the mighty flood;*
> *Louder still and louder*
> *Praise the precious Blood!*
>
> —76 SBH, 158 LH

PRAYER

Dear Christ, my Savior: May your death on the cross be precious to me all my life. Amen. The Lord's Prayer.

Wednesday   *The Second Article*

". . . and his innocent suffering . . ."

Crucifixion was a horrible and disgraceful form of death. It was used for the worst kinds of criminals and those who revolted against the government. It often took many hours before death brought a merciful end to the sufferings of the victims. It was bad enough that a man who was guilty should be tortured in such a way; but for a man who was innocent to die such a death is almost more than we can bear to think about. Our Lord was absolutely innocent of any crime against either the government or any individual, yet the Jewish priests and leaders hated him because they were afraid of the truth which he preached. They were afraid that he would win the people away from them, and that they would no longer hold their high offices. So they demanded that the Roman governor, Pilate, have him crucified. And so, for our sake, Jesus, who was innocent, allowed himself to be put to death as the worst of criminals.

The Bible tells us that Jesus was glad to die for us:

> . . . looking to Jesus the pioneer and perfecter of our faith, who for the joy that was set before him endured the cross, despising the shame, and is seated at the right hand of the throne of God.
>
> —Hebrews 12:2

We express our thanks to Jesus for his love to us in this hymn:

> *What language shall I borrow*
> *To thank thee, dearest friend,*
> *For this thy dying sorrow,*
> *Thy pity without end?*
> *O make me thine for ever,*
> *And should I fainting be,*
> *Lord, let me never, never*
> *Outlive my love to thee.*
>
> —88 SBH, 172 LH

PRAYER

Dear Christ, my Savior: Help me to find joy in serving you as you did find joy in dying for me. Amen. The Lord's Prayer.

". . . and his innocent suffering . . ."

There is much suffering in the world caused by death and sickness, poverty and disease, hatred and greed. If you lose a friend, or a loved one dies, you suffer. If you have been seriously ill, you know what suffering means. Parents often suffer sorrow or disappointment over their children. These things give us some idea of how our Lord suffered. But we will never fully understand what his suffering was like because we are only human. We suffer for ourselves or for a few loved ones at most, but Jesus suffered for the whole world, for all people. He felt the sins of all men everywhere and in every age. He felt all the poverty and the cruelty and hatred and greed of the whole world in his own heart, because he was God, and all men are his children.

The most wonderful description of Christ's sufferings for us comes from the Prophet Isaiah:

> He was despised and rejected by men;
>   a man of sorrows, and acquainted with grief;
> and as one from whom men hide their faces
>   he was despised, and we esteemed him not.
>
> Surely he has borne our griefs and carried
>   our sorrows;
> yet we esteemed him stricken, smitten by God,
>   and afflicted.
> But he was wounded for our transgressions,
>   he was bruised for our iniquities;
> upon him was the chastisement that made us whole,
>   and with his stripes we are healed.
>   —Isaiah 53:3-5

We remember Jesus' suffering in this Lenten hymn:

> *O Lamb of God most holy!*
> *Who on the Cross didst suffer,*
> *And patient still and lowly,*
> *Thyself to scorn didst offer;*
> *Our sins by thee were taken,*
> *Or hope had us forsaken:*
> *Have mercy on us, Jesus!*
>   —70 SBH

PRAYER

Dear Christ, my Savior: May your suffering for me make me more willing to undergo hardships to help others. Amen. The Lord's Prayer.

124

Friday   *The Second Article*

"... and his innocent ... death ..."

Jesus has redeemed me by his death. None of us will ever be able to understand fully what that means. It is too great a miracle, and we must believe it because our Lord says it is so. But we can have at least some idea of how we are saved from sin and everlasting death by Jesus' death on the cross. We have said before that, because we have broken God's moral law time after time, we deserve death, for God is just, and he must punish wrongdoers. Otherwise he would not be an honest God. But God is also love, and so he came in the form of a man to take upon himself our sin and the punishment and the death that by all rights we deserved. He gave his own life. No human could die to save other human beings from their sins because we are all sinful. Only the Son of God himself, whose life was perfect, could die in order that our sins might be forgiven and that we might live forever in heaven.

The Lord's Supper should always remind us that Jesus died to save us:

> Now as they were eating, Jesus took bread, and blessed, and broke it, and gave it to the disciples and said, "Take, eat; this is my body." And he took a cup, and when he had given thanks he gave it to them, saying, "Drink of it, all of you; for this is my blood of the covenant, which is poured out for many for the forgiveness of sins."
>
> —Matthew 26:26-28

In this hymn we sing that only Christ's death can save us:

> *Thy death, not mine, O Christ,*
> *Has paid the ransom due;*
> *Ten thousand deaths like mine*
> *Would have been all too few.*
> *To whom, save Thee,*
> *Who canst alone*
> *For sin atone*
> *Lord, shall I flee?*
>
> —68 CSB

PRAYER

Dear Christ, my Savior: I thank you that you have done for me what no one else can do. Amen. The Lord's Prayer.

"... and his innocent ... death ..."

We say that Jesus took our sins upon himself, and that by his death all our sins are forgiven. How can that be? Again it is almost impossible to explain something so profound in human language, but we can understand it in a way. It is as if you suddenly became angry and punched your friend in the eye, but instead of hitting you back your friend would say, "I know you couldn't control yourself; I forgive you." It wouldn't have meant very much if your friend had forgiven you for hitting someone else. That would have been too easy—"no skin off my nose," as we say. But when he forgives you for hitting him, that is another matter! And so it is with Jesus. He did not ask God to forgive people for what they did to someone else, but for what they did to him. They called him a liar and a drunkard and a worker of the devil; they hated him and tried to throw him over a cliff. They tried to stone him to death; they spit in his face, they made fun of him, and they pushed a crown of thorns on his head. Finally they nailed him to a cross. They committed every kind of sin against Jesus that man can commit, including the worst sin of all: murder. But after men had done their worst to him, he lifted up his eyes to heaven and said, "Father, forgive them, for they know not what they do." That is why God forgives us. That is why Christ died.

Jesus tells us in his own words why he willingly died on the cross:

> Greater love has no man than this, that a man lay down his
> life for his friends.
> —John 15:13

This hymn tells us that Jesus is our greatest friend:

> *Which of all our friends, to save us,*
> *   Could or would have shed his blood?*
> *But this Saviour died to have us*
> *   Reconciled in him to God;*
> *This was boundless love indeed;*
> *Jesus is a friend in need.*
> —456 SBH

PRAYER

Dear Christ, my Savior: I thank you for being my friend and forgiving all my sins. Amen. The Lord's Prayer.

"... that I may be his own ..."

It is not an easy matter for Christ to be our Lord and for us to be his children. All day long, and every day, the devil is trying in all the ways he knows to stop us from belonging to God. He tries to stop us by making us doubt our faith and leading us to wonder if there really is a God who sent his only Son to save us. The devil tries to stop us from being God's children by putting all kinds of temptation in our way to draw us away from God. He tries to make us like the movies, television, sports, and parties better than we like church, so that we find as many excuses as we can to stay away from Sunday school and league and not study our catechetical lessons. But Jesus suffered and died and rose again so that, if we believe in him, we will have strength enough to stand against the devil and his temptations and follow God's will and be his children.

St. Paul tells us in these beautiful words that we are God's children because of Christ:

> Blessed be the God and Father of our Lord Jesus Christ, who has blessed us in Christ with every spiritual blessing in the heavenly places, even as he chose us in him before the foundation of the world, that we should be holy and blameless before him. He destined us in love to be his sons through Jesus Christ, according to the purpose of his will, to the praise of his glorious grace which he freely bestowed on us in the Beloved. In him we have redemption through his blood, the forgiveness of our trespasses, according to the riches of his grace which he lavished upon us.
> —Ephesians 1:3-8

In this hymn we ask God to let us be his children always:

Let me be thine forever,   *Preserve me from the mazes*
  My gracious God and Lord;   *Of error and distrust,*
May I forsake thee never,   *And I shall sing thy praises*
  Nor wander from thy word.   *Forever with the just.*

—506 SBH, 334 LH

PRAYER

Dear heavenly Father: I thank you that I am your child. Help me so to live that I will be yours forever. Amen. The Lord's Prayer.

Monday   *The Second Article*

"... that I may ... live under him ..."

People have given their loyalty to many kinds of rulers—kings, emperors, princes, dictators, presidents. Some of them have been good; many of them have been bad. But even the best have made many mistakes and caused much trouble in the world. Christians, no matter where they live, and no matter under what government, have only one true Lord and Leader: Jesus Christ. Christians are willing to obey and follow their human leaders so long as it does not mean going against Christ. When their human leaders go against Christ, Christians can no longer obey and follow. Christians have often suffered greatly for this, but our Lord has promised that whoever lives under him in this life will also live under him in the next life, forever.

Jesus tells us that he himself will prepare his kingdom for those who love him and are true to him:

> In my Father's house are many rooms; if it were not so, would I have told you that I go to prepare a place for you? And when I go and prepare a place for you, I will come again and will take you to myself, that where I am you may be also.
>
> —John 14:2-3

This hymn tells about Christ's being our King in the next life:

> *King of glory, reign for ever;*
> *Thine an everlasting crown;*
> *Nothing from Thy love shall sever*
> *Those whom Thou hast made Thine own;*
> *Happy objects of Thy grace,*
> *Destined to behold Thy face.*
>
> —133 CSB

PRAYER

Dear Lord Jesus: Help me to be your true and faithful servant in this life so that I can live under you in heaven. Amen. The Lord's Prayer.

Tuesday   *The Second Article*

"... live under him in his kingdom ..."

Just as there have been many kinds of rulers in the world, so there have been many kinds of kingdoms. And, as in the case of the rulers, some have been good, and many have been bad. The best of them, including all forms of government, have been far from perfect. Christians, no matter where they live, are all members of the same kingdom: the kingdom of our Lord Jesus Christ. Right now that kingdom is a spiritual one; it is in our hearts. The kingdom grows every time another person comes to believe in Christ. But our Lord has promised us that if we believe in him and his salvation for us, we will be members of his kingdom, which he will bring when he comes again in power and glory. We will be able to see it and live in it.

One of the many verses in the Bible which tells about Christ's coming again to set up his kingdom is this one in the Gospel of Mark:

> ... and the stars will be falling from heaven, and the powers in the heavens will be shaken. And then they will see the Son of man coming in clouds with great power and glory. And then he will send out the angels, and gather his elect from the four winds, from the ends of the earth to the ends of heaven.
>
> —Mark 13:25-27

Christ and his kingdom are praised in this hymn:

> *Blessing and honor, and glory and power,*
> *Wisdom, and riches, and strength evermore,*
> *Give ye to him who our battle hath won,*
> *Whose are the kingdom, the crown, and the throne.*
> —166 SBH

PRAYER

Dear Lord Jesus: Help me to believe and live so that I may have a part in your kingdom. Amen. The Lord's Prayer.

Wednesday   *The Second Article*

". . . and serve him in everlasting . . ."

It is hard for us to imagine what "everlasting" means, because nothing in this world lasts forever. No matter how big and solid men make their buildings, in time they will all become like the Greek and Roman buildings: ruins where tourists poke around for souvenirs. No matter how hard kings and dictators may try to build governments that will last forever, none ever has; most governments have died with their leaders. And we know that our bodies do not last forever, even though men have tried many ways to lengthen human life. But God promises us that in his kingdom there will be no decay, no growing old, no death. By rising from the dead on Easter morning he showed us that he has power over life and death, and that death itself is not everlasting. Some day, for those of us who believe in him, death will be over and we will live together with our Lord. Our life will have no end. It will last forever.

The Apostle John gives us one of the most famous Bible passages about everlasting life:

> For God so loved the world that he gave his only Son, that whoever believes in him should not perish but have eternal life.
>
> —John 3:16

In the *Service Book and Hymnal* there is a section entitled "Life Everlasting" from which this hymn is quoted:

> *For ever with the Lord!*
> *Amen, so let it be;*
> *Life from the dead is in that word,*
> *'Tis immortality.*

> *For ever with the Lord!*
> *Father, if 'tis thy will,*
> *The promise of that faithful word*
> *E'en here to me fulfill.*
>
> —590 SBH, 616 LH

PRAYER

Dear Lord Jesus: I give you thanks for your promise of life everlasting in which my greatest hopes and joys will come true. Amen. The Lord's Prayer.

Thursday   *The Second Article*

"... and serve him in everlasting righteousness ..."

No one is absolutely sure just what heaven will be like in every detail. But we can be sure of some things about it. For one thing, it will be a wonderful place—more wonderful than we can even imagine. We can be sure, too, that righteousness will rule in heaven. When a person is righteous, he does what is right, or he does God's will. We know that no human being on earth is all righteous, or is righteous all the time. Every hour of every day we go against God's will. That is why there is so much crime and misery and sorrow in our world. The best of us are righteous only a small part of the time, and most people do not even know God or try to do his will. But in heaven everyone will be righteous and will be doing God's will all the time. We can only guess how happy and beautiful such a life will be, and hope and pray we will be with those who are going to serve God "in everlasting righteousness."

St. Paul writes to his helper Timothy about everlasting righteousness:

> I have fought the good fight, I have finished the race, I have kept the faith. Henceforth there is laid up for me the crown of righteousness, which the Lord, the righteous judge, will award to me on that Day, and not only to me but also to all who have loved his appearing.
>
> —2 Timothy 4:7-8

We sing about this crown of righteousness in the following hymn:

> *So may we join Thy Name to bless,*
> *Thy grace adore, Thy power confess,*
> *From sin and strife to flee;*
> *One is our calling, one our name,*
> *The end of all our hopes the same!*
> *A crown of life with Thee.*
>
> —269, CSB, 412 LH

PRAYER

Dear Lord Jesus: Help me to fight the good fight, to finish the race, to keep the faith, so that I may be with you forever. Amen. The Lord's Prayer.

". . . and serve him in everlasting . . . innocence . . ."

We say that a little child is innocent, and we mean that he does not know anything evil. The reason that there seems to be such a difference between the face of a child and that of a grown-up person is that the grown-up knows what evil is. He has done evil, he has thought evil, and he has spoken evil. A person's face is a mirror of his personality. But the little child has not yet known, or done, or thought, or spoken evil, and his face is therefore innocent. The first people God created were innocent, like children, and did not know what evil was. But as soon as they disobeyed God, they tasted evil, because that is what evil is: disobeying God. Ever since that time, evil has ruled the hearts of men, and not even the most sincere Christians are free from it. But in heaven we will again be as God intended us to be. We will not know or think or speak or do any evil, but serve him in everlasting innocence.

White is the color of purity and innocence in this Bible passage. St. John gives us a look at heaven, where we will serve God in innocence:

> After this I looked, and behold, a great multitude which no man could number, from every nation, from all tribes and peoples and tongues, standing before the throne and before the Lamb, clothed in white robes, with palm branches in their hands, and crying out with a loud voice, "Salvation belongs to our God who sits upon the throne, and to the Lamb!"
>
> —Revelation 7:9-10

We ask God in this hymn to make us pure and innocent:

> *Finish then thy new creation,*
> *Pure and spotless let us be;*
> *Let us see thy great salvation*
> *Perfectly restored in thee!*
> *Changed from glory into glory,*
> *Till in heaven we take our place,*
> *Till we cast our crowns before thee,*
> *Lost in wonder, love, and praise.*
>
> —397 SBH, 351 LH 276 CSB

PRAYER

Dear Lord Jesus: Help me to grow in purity and goodness in this life so that I may be with those who will serve you forever. Amen. The Lord's Prayer.

". . . and serve him in everlasting . . . blessedness . . ."

Blessedness means true happiness, not the kind that comes from everyday pleasures, but the kind that comes from inside a person and is a part of him. As long as we are on this earth, we are never fully blessed. There is always some disappointment, some discouragement, some sadness, something not as it should be. In heaven there will be no pain or sorrow, no sin or death. Everything will be as it should be, as God intended it. No matter how hard we try to make it so, this world will never be perfect because people will never be perfect. We may be able, with God's help, to make our world better than it is, but only in heaven, in the life to come, will our hearts and minds be free of all unhappiness. Only then will we be able to serve God in everlasting blessedness.

Such blessedness is described by St. John in his vision of heaven:

> . . . and God himself will be with them; he will wipe away every tear from their eyes, and death shall be no more, neither shall there be mourning nor crying nor pain any more, for the former things have passed away.
>
> —Revelation 21:3-4

We sing about the blessedness of heaven in this hymn:

> *Saints robed in white before the shining throne*
> *Their joyful anthems raise,*
> *Till heaven's glad halls are echoing with the tone*
> *Of that great hymn of praise,*
> *And all its host rejoices,*
> *And all its blessed throng*
> *Unite their myriad voices*
> *In one eternal song.*
>
> —588 SBH

PRAYER

Dear Lord Jesus: Help me so to live in this life that I may enjoy the true happiness of heaven. Amen. The Lord's Prayer.

Sunday   *The Second Article*

". . . just as he is risen from the dead . . ."

Last week our devotions had to do with the promises of Christ: that we would live under him in his kingdom for ever and ever. When someone makes us a promise that is very important, we want to feel sure that the promise will be kept. How do we know Christ will keep his promise to us of everlasting life with him? We know it because of what happened on that first Easter morning some 1900 years ago. We have the record in the New Testament by actual eye-witnesses that Christ, who had been crucified, dead, and buried, had come to life again. These same witnesses tell us that he was with them for 40 days afterward and ate and talked and walked with them before he went back to heaven. Because Christ rose from the dead, we can believe his promise to us.

Jesus' resurrection is connected with our eternal life in these words of St. Paul:

> If the Spirit of him who raised Jesus from the dead dwells in you, he who raised Christ Jesus from the dead will give life to your mortal bodies also through his Spirit which dwells in you.
>
> —Romans 8:11

Easter hymns are joyful because Jesus' rising from the dead assures us of our own resurrection:

> *Christ is risen, we are risen!*
> *Shed upon us heavenly grace,*
> *Rain and dew and gleams of glory*
> *From the brightness of thy face;*
> *That we, Lord, with hearts in heaven,*
> *Here on earth may fruitful be,*
> *And by angel hands be gathered*
> *And be ever safe with thee.*
>
> —108 SBH

PRAYER

Dear Jesus, my risen Lord: I thank you that you have helped me to believe in eternal life by rising from the dead. Amen. The Lord's Prayer.

"... just as he is risen from the dead ..."

Not only did Christ show us that he could conquer death by rising again, but he showed us what kind of bodies we will have in the life after death. When Jesus appeared to his disciples after his death, he looked the same to them as he had always looked. He even asked his disciples to touch him to be sure they were not seeing a ghost, and he sat down with them and ate.

But his body was not the same as it was before, even though it looked the same. Before, it had been a physical body, limited by the laws of nature. Now it was a spiritual body, and it was above natural law. After his resurrection Jesus went from one place to another, but no one saw him come or go. He came into the room where the disciples were hiding, even though the doors were locked and no one let him in. After the disciples at Emmaus had recognized him at the breaking of the bread, he disappeared before their very eyes. After Christ had said good-by to his disciples and commanded them to preach the gospel to all the world, he disappeared into heaven. Because Christ rose from the dead and appeared to his disciples for 40 days after his resurrection, we know that some day our own bodies will be raised and made immortal.

We learn from the New Testament that our human bodies will be changed into bodies like Christ's:

> So is it with the resurrection of the dead. What is sown is perishable, what is raised is imperishable. It is sown in dishonor, it is raised in glory. It is sown in weakness, it is raised in power. It is sown a physical body, it is raised a spiritual body. If there is a physical body, there is also a spiritual body. —1 Corinthians 15:42-44

In this Easter hymn we sing about being made like Christ in the life hereafter:

> *Soar we now where Christ hath led,*
> *Following our exalted Head:*
> *Made like him, like him we rise;*
> *Ours the cross, the grave, the skies.*
> —91 SBH, 193 LH, 111 CSB

PRAYER

Dear Jesus, my risen Lord: I thank you for the assurance of a real body and a real life after death. Amen. The Lord's Prayer.

"... just as he ... lives ..."

It ought to be a great comfort to us, and it ought to give us courage to know that the God we believe in and worship really lives. Think of the millions of people in the world, even today, who worship idols of wood and stone and metal that have been made with their own hands. These gods live only in the minds of these poor people, who are taught from childhood to worship them. Other people try to make gods out of their leaders, who are here today and gone tomorrow. In India the people worship cows, and in Egypt almost all the animals and birds are worshiped. In Germany the cross was taken down from the walls of schools and churches, and the picture of Hitler and the emblem of the swastika were put up instead.

As Christians we worship the real God, the one true God, who has created us and all that exists, who has revealed himself to us in the person of Christ, and who lives now and forevermore.

In the Greek city of Athens, St. Paul tried to tell the people about the true, living God:

> The God who made the world and everything in it, being Lord of heaven and earth, does not live in shrines made by man, nor is he served by human hands, as though he needed anything, since he himself gives to all men life and breath and everything.
>
> —Acts 17:24-25

In this famous hymn we sing about how much it means to us to know that our God is a living God:

> *He lives, all glory to his Name;*
> *He lives, my Saviour, still the same;*
> *What joy the blest assurance gives:*
> *I know that my Redeemer lives!*
>
> —387 SBH

PRAYER

Dear Jesus, our risen Lord: I am thankful that I can worship the true God because you have made him known to me. Amen. The Lord's Prayer.

"... just as he ... lives ..."

Although it is true that Christ is our ever-living Lord, it would not be enough simply to have him in heaven, at the right hand of God. The most reassuring thing of all about our Lord is that he lives in our hearts. That is how we really come to know him. That is the only way he can change our hearts and save us from our sins. Christ wants to enter every heart, if only we will let him in. And when he comes he brings love—love for God and love for our fellow man. When we let Christ into our hearts he makes it possible for us to obey the greatest commandment of all: "You shall love the Lord your God with all your heart . . . and your neighbor as yourself." When Christ lives in our hearts we will love God more than anything the world has to offer, and we will put church first, before all the other things we do. Then we will think of poor and suffering people everywhere as our neighbors and try to help them as we would want to be helped.

The Apostle Paul says that Christ not only lives, but he lives in our hearts, making it possible for us to lead Christian lives:

> I have been crucified with Christ; it is no longer I who live, but Christ who lives in me; and the life I now live in the flesh I live by faith in the Son of God, who loved me and gave himself for me.
> —Galatians 2:20

We ask in this hymn that we may let Jesus live in our hearts:

> *O let thy love constrain us*
> *To give our hearts to thee;*
> *Let nothing please or pain us,*
> *Apart, O Lord, from thee;*
> *Our joy, our one endeavor,*
> *Through suffering, conflict, shame,*
> *To serve thee, gracious Saviour,*
> *And magnify thy Name.*
> —401 SBH, 363 CSB

PRAYER

Dear Jesus, our risen Lord: I pray that you will come into my heart and be the King of my life. Amen. The Lord's Prayer.

Thursday *The Second Article*

"... just as he ... rules ..."

Every person's heart is ruled by someone or something. Millions of people are ruled by what we call communism—a religion that makes the state a god. The devil rules many hearts through a love for money, a love for alcohol, or a love for crime of any kind. Leaders' hearts have often been ruled by a love for power, and they usually are able to get some scientists, business men, professors, and even ministers to go along with them. But there is only one ruler who reigns in the heart of a true Christian: Jesus Christ. When Christ rules in our hearts, there is no room for other kinds of rulers. It is only when Christ reigns in our hearts that we really are free, free to be and act and think and believe as we ought. Christ is truth, and the truth makes us free.

We learn from the New Testament that true knowledge and peace come to a person when Christ rules in his heart:

> . . . and that Christ may dwell in your hearts through faith; that you, being rooted and grounded in love, may have power to comprehend with all the saints what is the breadth and length and height and depth, and to know the love of Christ which surpasses knowledge, that you may be filled with all the fullness of God.
>
> —Ephesians 3:17-19

In this Advent hymn we ask Christ to come and rule in our hearts:

> *Born thy people to deliver,*
> *Born a child, and yet a king;*
> *Born to reign in us forever,*
> *Now thy gracious kingdom bring.*
> *By thine own eternal Spirit*
> *Rule in all our hearts alone;*
> *By thine all-sufficient merit*
> *Raise us to thy glorious throne.*
>
> —5 SBH, 12 CSB

PRAYER

Come into my heart, Lord Jesus. Come in today. Come in to stay. Come into my heart, Lord Jesus. Amen. The Lord's Prayer.

"... just as he ... rules ..."

Christ rules over our hearts in a spiritual way now, but the time is coming when he will not only reign over our hearts, but over the world and the heavens and the whole creation. When he comes again, with power and glory, the reign of the devil in the world will be over, and Christ alone will be King. Then, instead of sorrow and suffering, there will be joy; instead of hatred and greed, there will be love; instead of war, there will be peace. Christ has promised us that if we are faithful to him now in this life, no matter how hard it may be, then we will rule with him when he reigns over all things. Christians have a King who is more powerful than any earthly ruler has ever been or ever will be. Earthly rulers have tried to conquer and reign over the world, and some have been successful for a short time. But Jesus Christ our Lord, when he comes again, will have all power in heaven and earth as his own. There will be no other rulers but him.

This Bible verse looks forward to the time when Christ will reign over all creation:

> Therefore God has highly exalted him and bestowed on him the name which is above every name, that at the name of Jesus every knee should bow, in heaven and on earth and under the earth, and every tongue confess that Jesus Christ is Lord, to the glory of God the Father.
> —Philippians 2:9-11

There are many hymns in which we sing about the day when Jesus will be Lord of all:

> *The highest place that heaven affords*
> *Is his, is his by right,*
> *The King of kings, and Lord of lords,*
> *And heaven's eternal Light;*
>
> *The joy of all who dwell above,*
> *The joy of all below,*
> *To whom he manifests his love*
> *And grants his Name to know.*
> —439 SBH

PRAYER

Dear Jesus, our risen Lord: Help me to be faithful until that day when you will rule over heaven and earth forever. Amen. The Lord's Prayer.

". . . just as he . . . rules eternally."

The great hope of the Christian is eternal, everlasting life with God. It is only because we can believe in eternal life after death that our present life makes sense. If there were not life after death, it would be hard to find a reason for our being here at all. Many people go through this life with nothing but pain and misery. Many others are cut off by death right in the middle of their happiest or most successful years. If death were really the end, life would simply have no meaning.

That is why some people who do not believe in God or eternal life spend their lives in crime, or in eating, drinking, and trying to be merry. They do not try to make any sense out of life, because they can't.

Christians, however, know that the only thing that matters in this life is that we build up a strong faith in God, that we know him and come to love him, so that in the next life we will be with him when he rules eternally.

St. Paul reminds the early Christians that their lives have a purpose because they believe in eternal life:

> For those who sleep sleep at night, and those who get drunk are drunk at night. But, since we belong to the day, let us be sober, and put on the breastplate of faith and love, and for a helmet the hope of salvation. For God has not destined us for wrath, but to obtain salvation through our Lord Jesus Christ, who died for us so that whether we wake or sleep we might live with him.
>
> —1 Thessalonians 5:7-10

This famous hymn reminds us that heaven is our real goal and purpose in life:

> *Awake, my soul, stretch every nerve,*
> *And press with vigor on;*
> *A heavenly race demands thy zeal,*
> *And an immortal crown.*
>
> —552 SBH, 380 CSB

PRAYER

Dear Jesus, our risen Lord: Help me to keep the goal of heaven always in my mind and heart. Amen. The Lord's Prayer.

"I believe that I cannot by my own understanding . . . believe in Jesus Christ my Lord . . ."

There are many things that our minds can reason out. Every time you do an arithmetic problem or figure out a problem in chemistry or do a puzzle, you are making use of your powers of reason. But there are many things that our minds cannot reason out. There is a certain limit past which our minds can't go, no matter how smart we may be. Our minds by themselves could never bring us to believe in Jesus Christ. Our minds by themselves could never figure out why God would send his only Son into the world as a man in order to save us from our sins. God has to tell us that himself, through his Word, before we would even know about it. That is why millions of people don't believe in Jesus—they have never heard about him and can't find out about him through their own reason.

The Bible tells us that we can't know God through our own wisdom:

> For since, in the wisdom of God, the world did not know God through wisdom, it pleased God through the folly of what we preach to save those who believe. For Jews demand signs and Greeks seek wisdom, but we preach Christ crucified, a stumbling-block to Jews and folly to Gentiles, but to those who are called, both Jews and Greeks, Christ the power of God and the wisdom of God.
>
> —1 Corinthians 1:21-25

The reason for sending out missionaries is that people cannot come to Jesus by their own reason or wisdom. They have to be told about him, as we sing in this great hymn:

> *Proclaim to every people, tongue, and nation*
> *That God, in whom they live and move, is love:*
> *Tell how he stooped to save his lost creation,*
> *And died on earth that man might live above.*
> *Publish glad tidings, tidings of peace;*
> *Tidings of Jesus, redemption and release.*
> —314 SBH, 224 CSB

PRAYER

Dear heavenly Father: Help me to trust in your Word and the power of your Holy Spirit rather than in my own reason alone. Amen. The Lord's Prayer.

"I believe that I cannot by my own . . . effort believe in Jesus Christ my Lord . . ."

In this case effort means willpower. We can't make ourselves believe in Jesus Christ by sheer willpower. We may think we can, but we really can't. The reason is that the devil is at work in us to see that we don't believe. That is why, even with a church on almost every corner, nearly half the people of the United States do not believe in him. When it comes to actually making a decision to believe in him, they can't go through with it. Even though many persons agree they ought to believe in Jesus Christ, still they can't get themselves to do it by their own willpower. The devil is too strong for our wills, but if we open our hearts to the Holy Spirit, he will change our wills and make it possible for us to believe.

The Bible teaches us that we need help in order to believe:

> Therefore I want you to understand that no one speaking by the Spirit of God ever says, "Jesus be cursed!" and no one can say "Jesus is Lord" except by the Holy Spirit.
> —1 Corinthians 12:3

In this hymn we ask the Holy Spirit to give us strength to believe:

> O strong Defence, O holy Light!
> That we may know our God aright,
> And call him Father from the heart,
> The word of life and truth impart.
> Make us to trust in God alone,
> And Jesus for our Master own,
> His yoke and teaching ne'er to change
> For other doctrines new and strange.
> —122 SBH

PRAYER

Dear heavenly Father: Help me to trust in your Word and the power of your Holy Spirit rather than in my own strength. In Jesus' name. Amen. The Lord's Prayer.

Tuesday   *The Third Article*

"I believe that I cannot by my own understanding or effort . . . come to him."

When we really believe in something, we do more than simply say to ourselves, "Yes, that's right!" We also do something about it. We believe in education, so we go to school. If your parents really believe in democracy, they vote. If we really believe in a certain newspaper or magazine, we buy it. If we really believe in Jesus Christ, we will do something about that too: We will come to him; we will try to do his will; we will try to obey his commandments. But here again the devil tries to stop us. That is why many people agree with Christ's teachings, but do not follow them and do not give themselves to Christ. Here again, the Holy Spirit must enter our hearts and give us strength to come to Christ.

This Bible verse says that we can't come to God without being led by his Spirit:

For all who are led by the Spirit of God are sons of God.
—Romans 8:14

In this hymn we ask the Holy Spirit to lead us to Christ:

Lead us to Christ, the living way,
Nor let us from his pastures stray;
Lead us to holiness, the road
That we must take to dwell with God.
—127 SBH, 150 CSB

PRAYER

Dear heavenly Father: May your Holy Spirit enter my heart and bring me closer to you each day. In Jesus' name. Amen. The Lord's Prayer.

143

"But the Holy Spirit has called me through the Gospel . . ."

If it were not for the Gospel, or God's message of salvation, we could never come to believe in God or do his will, because our own reason and willpower are not strong enough. But the Holy Spirit is in God's Word—in the Bible—and when we read it or hear it, he begins to work on us to bring us to God. It is like any other invitation. We do not know about it until we read or hear it. Then we think about coming. That is why it is so important for the church to send missionaries into all parts of the world so that those who do not know about God's invitation to come to him may hear it and read it, and that the Holy Spirit may call them or invite them to share in the salvation which Christ has made possible for all men.

The importance of getting the Gospel message to people is stressed in this passage from the New Testament:

> For, "every one who calls upon the name of the Lord will be saved." But how are men to call upon him in whom they have not believed? And how are they to believe in him of whom they have never heard? And how are they to hear without a preacher?
>
> —Romans 10:13-15

In this hymn we ask the Holy Spirit to speak to us through God's Word:

> *Eternal Spirit, who dost speak*
> *To mind and conscience still,*
> *That we, in this our day, may seek*
> *To do our Father's will:*
> *Thy word of life impart,*
> *That tells of Christ, the living Way;*
> *Give us the quiet humble heart*
> *To hear and to obey.*
>
> —251 SBH

PRAYER

Dear heavenly Father: I thank you for your Gospel and its message of salvation. Help me to bring it to others. In Jesus' name. Amen. The Lord's Prayer.

"But the Holy Spirit has ... enlightened me with his gifts ..."

One of the worst things that sin does is to darken our minds so that we cannot know or love or understand God by ourselves, even when we read or hear his Word. But God's Holy Spirit enlightens our dark minds so that when we read or hear the Word, we can understand it. People who keep the Holy Spirit from their hearts think that God's Word is foolishness. They do not understand it, and they do not want to. They are like a child who throws away a map to a lost treasure because he cannot read it. The salvation that our Lord offers us is the treasure, the Word of God is the map, and the Holy Spirit is the guide who shows us how to understand the map. Without his enlightenment, the treasure is lost to us.

Jesus promises us that the Holy Spirit will enlighten our minds to understand God's Word:

> When the Spirit of truth comes, he will guide you into all the truth; for he will not speak on his own authority, but whatever he hears he will speak, and he will declare to you the things that are to come.
>
> —John 16:13

We ask for the Holy Spirit's gifts of enlightenment in this hymn:

> *Come, Holy Ghost, our souls inspire*
> *And lighten with celestial fire;*
> *Thou the anointing Spirit art*
> *Who dost thy seven-fold gifts impart.*
> *Praise to thy eternal merit,*
> *Father, Son, and Holy Spirit.*
>
> —117 SBH

PRAYER

Dear heavenly Father: I thank you that my mind has been enlightened to understand your Word and to love you. Amen. The Lord's Prayer.

145

"But the Holy Spirit has . . . sanctified . . . me . . ."

To sanctify means to make holy. Anything that is holy belongs to God. So the Holy Spirit makes us holy by bringing us to God and helping us to belong to God. People who have not been sanctified or made holy by God's Spirit do not belong to him. They do not want anything to do with him. Other people should be able to tell whether or not we are sanctified Christians, whether or not we belong to God. They should be able to tell it by the way we talk. Does our speech belong to God, or do we have to be ashamed of it? People should be able to tell by the things we do. Do our actions belong to God, or do we have to be ashamed of them? The Holy Spirit can make us holy only if we let him take over our thoughts and speech and actions and make them the tools which God can use to carry on the work of his kingdom.

St. Paul tells what a sanctified life is like:

> But the fruit of the Spirit is love, joy, peace, patience, kindness, goodness, faithfulness, gentleness, self-control; against such there is no law.
>
> —Galatians 5:22-23

We ask in this hymn that God's Spirit will make it possible for us to live holy lives:

> *Lord, let thy Spirit, new love and life bestowing,*
> *Create a holy heart my breast within;*
> *That I, into my Saviour's likeness growing,*
> *May bear his image through a world of sin.*
> —128 SBH

PRAYER

Dear heavenly Father: Help me to live a holy life in thought, word, and deed and to bring others to you by my example. In Jesus' name. Amen. The Lord's Prayer.

"But the Holy Spirit has . . . kept me in true faith."

Our faith is not something that stays with us automatically. We need God's help to keep it, or we may lose it. The devil is always trying to make our faith weaker or to make us lose it altogether. We are not strong enough to keep it by ourselves. We must have the help of God's Holy Spirit. We must let him take over our lives and guide us. Every hour of every day we must be on guard against losing our faith. We must pray and read our Bibles and go to Sunday school and church, because it is through these things that the Holy Spirit speaks to us and works with us to keep our faith and to make it strong.

St. Paul tells us that we must fight the devil and depend on God's help to keep our faith:

> Put on the whole armor of God, that you may be able to stand against the wiles of the devil. For we are not contending against flesh and blood, but against the principalities, against the powers, against the world rulers of this present darkness, against the spiritual hosts of wickedness in the heavenly places. Therefore take the whole armor of God, that you may be able to withstand in the evil day, and having done all, to stand.
>
> —Ephesians 6:11-13

In this hymn we ask the Holy Spirit to keep us in the faith all our lives:

> *O mighty Rock, O Source of life!*
> *Let thy dear word, 'mid doubt and strife,*
>   *Be so within us burning,*
> *That we be faithful unto death*
> *In thy pure love and holy faith,*
>   *From thee true wisdom learning.*
>   *Lord, thy graces*
> *On us shower; by thy power*
>   *Christ confessing,*
> *Let us win his grace and blessing.*
>
> —120 SBH

PRAYER

Dear heavenly Father: Give me strength through your Holy Spirit to keep my faith and to grow stronger in it day by day. In Jesus' name. Amen. The Lord's Prayer.

"... the whole Christian church on earth ..."

What comes to your mind when you hear the word "church"? Most of us will say that a building with a steeple on it comes to mind. Many Roman Catholics probably think of St. Peter's Church in Rome or of the Pope. But the real meaning of the word "church" is not a building or stained glass windows or organ music. "Church" means a body of people who believe in Jesus Christ. They may live in America or China or Germany; but wherever there are people who believe in Jesus Christ as their Lord and Savior, there is a part of the true church. We have come to call the buildings where the congregation meets for worship the church. But Christ did not come to earth to put up church buildings. He came to plant the Christian faith in the hearts of people. His disciples are still carrying on that work today. Christ's church is wherever people believe in him and worship him, whether they do so in a building or not. Christian people are the church.

Here is a description of the early Christian church in the time of the apostles:

> And all who believed were together and had all things in common; and they sold their possessions and goods and distributed them to all, as any had need. And day by day, attending the temple together and breaking bread in their homes, they partook of food with glad and generous hearts, praising God and having favor with all the people. And the Lord added to their number day by day those who were being saved.
>
> —Acts 2:44-47

In this hymn we sing about the fact that we are the church:

> *We are God's house of living stones,*
> *Built for his own habitation;*
> *He fills our hearts, his humble thrones,*
> *Granting us life and salvation;*
> *Were two or three to seek his face,*
> *He in their midst would show his grace,*
> *Blessings upon them bestowing.*
>
> —151 SBH

PRAYER

Dear Jesus, Lord of the church: May I be counted as one of those who are true members of the true church, the body of Christ. Amen. The Lord's Prayer.

148

Monday   *The Third Article*

"... the whole Christian church on earth ..."

A question comes to our minds when we talk about the church. If the church is the body of those who believe in Jesus Christ, why are there so many different kinds of churches? If the people in all these churches believe in Christ, why do we have to have Methodist churches and Lutheran churches and Baptist churches and all the rest? Why are there even different kinds of Lutheran churches?

One answer is that there are many kinds of people. People are different according to race, according to bringing up, and according to their positions in life. We cannot expect that with such differences all people would want to worship in the same way, in the same kind of church, even if all of them were Christian. The important thing is whether they really are Christian and whether they do believe in Jesus Christ as their Savior and don't look down on each other for worshiping in different ways.

As time goes on and the world gets to be more "one world," the differences of race and language become less important and more church groups get together. Every year such "mergers" are taking place in different parts of the world.

Jesus prays that those who believe in him may be one in spirit, no matter who or where they are:

> I do not pray for these only, but also for those who are to believe in me through their word, that they may all be one; even as thou, Father, art in me, and I in thee, that they also may be in us...
>
> —John 17:20-21

This hymn says that Christ himself is the foundation of the true church in spite of its differences:

The Church's one foundation   From heaven he came and sought her
Is Jesus Christ her Lord;   To be his holy bride,
She is his new creation   With his own Blood he bought her,
By water and the word: And for her life he died.
—149 SBH, 473 LH, 198 CSB

PRAYER

Dear Jesus, Lord of the church: I pray that all people everywhere may be members of your true church. Amen. The Lord's Prayer.

"In the same way he calls . . ."

The Holy Spirit is at work throughout the whole world, calling people to become members of the body of Christ, which is his church. The Holy Spirit does this calling through those who are already Christians. That is missionary work, and it is the chief job that we as the church have to do.

We get into the habit of thinking that missionary work is supposed to be done by professional missionaries only. We forget that all of us are missionaries if we take our faith seriously. There are people where we work, in our classrooms, in our neighborhood, even in our own families, who must be invited to become members of the church, the body of those who believe in Christ. That is the only way the church can grow. That is the only way the Holy Spirit can make his call heard: if you and I and all others who call themselves Christians do our part as missionaries.

Jesus commands us to call others into his church:

> Go therefore and make disciples of all nations, baptizing them in the name of the Father and of the Son and of the Holy Spirit, teaching them to observe all that I have commanded you; and lo, I am with you always, to the close of the age.
> —Matthew 28:19-20

We ask God in this hymn that his Word may be carried by us to people all over the world:

> *Spread, O spread, thou mighty word,*
> *Spread the kingdom of the Lord,*
> *That to earth's remotest bound*
> *Men may heed the joyful sound;*
>
> *Word of how the Father's will*
> *Made the world, and keeps it, still;*
> *How his only Son he gave,*
> *Man from sin and death to save.*
>
> —323 SBH

PRAYER

Dear Jesus, Lord of the church: Make me a missionary wherever I am to call people into your church. Amen. The Lord's Prayer.

"In the same way he . . . gathers . . ."

Those of us who are Christians and who make up the true church live in the world, like everyone else; but God does not want us to be a part of the world. The world is under the power of the devil, because most people have chosen him for their king instead of Christ, and they love evil instead of good. That is why we have already had two world wars in the 20th century and are afraid that another one may come. As Christians we cannot allow our hearts and souls to belong to such a place.

Christ has promised that when he comes again he will gather those who have been faithful to him—his church—and take them to live with him in his everlasting kingdom. Every Sunday Christians all over the earth are gathered together, apart from the world, in their houses of worship, just as they will be gathered some day in God's eternal house in heaven. In the meantime, it is our duty to gather as many souls as we can for God's church while we are in this life.

The apostles began right away, with the power of God's Spirit, to gather people into Christ's church. This passage is about Peter and his preaching in Jerusalem:

> And he testified with many other words and exhorted them, saying, "Save yourselves from this crooked generation." So those who received his word were baptized, and there were added that day about three thousand souls.
> —Acts 2:40-41

We sing in this hymn that we are happy to win others for Christ and his church:

> *Christ for the world we sing;*
> *The world to Christ we bring*
> *With loving zeal;*
> *The poor and them that mourn,*
> *The faint and over-borne,*
> *Sin-sick and sorrow-worn,*
> *Whom Christ doth heal.*
> —311 SBH, 218 CSB

PRAYER

Dear Jesus, Lord of the church: Help me by the power of your Spirit to bring some other person into church. Amen. The Lord's Prayer.

Thursday   *The Third Article*

"... in the same way he ... enlightens ..."

Whenever we learn anything our minds are enlightened. We say that we are "in the dark" about a certain matter until we get some information about it—until we get some "light" on the subject. We say that it is impossible to have a democracy without free public schools where people's minds can be enlightened so that they will be understanding and intelligent voters and office-holders.

But we do not often realize how important it is that we be enlightened about spiritual matters, about God who sent his Son for our salvation. That is the kind of enlightenment people all over the world need most of all. Millions of people are still in spiritual darkness and need the light of the Gospel: God's Word. The church is the only organization in the world through which the Holy Spirit can bring the light to the darkness of men's minds. It is only in the church that God's Word is preached and taught and brought to people in the Sacraments of the Lord's Supper and Baptism. God's church is truly the light of the world.

Jesus and "light" are often used together in the Bible:

> For it is the God who said, "Let light shine out of darkness," who has shone in our hearts to give the light of the knowledge of the glory of God in the face of Christ.
> —2 Corinthians 4:6

In this hymn we ask God that the church's light may shine throughout the world:

> *May her lamp of truth be bright;*
> *Bid her bear aloft its light*
> *Through the realms of heathen night:*
> *We beseech thee, hear us.*
>
> —153 SBH

PRAYER

Dear Jesus, Lord of the church: May my light so shine that others, seeing my good works, may glorify my Father who is in heaven. Amen. The Lord's Prayer.

Friday   *The Third Article*

"... in the same way he ... sanctifies ..."

We have said that to sanctify means to make holy and that to be holy means to belong to God. God is always working through his Spirit to make his church holier, to make it belong more to him, to make it more willing to carry out his will. It is only as members of God's church, his body of believers, that men can become holy, just as it is only through the church that men can be called and enlightened.

We may have an invitation to go to a certain place, and we may have all the information about the place, but we still may not want to go. Becoming holy, or sanctified, means that we actually go—we actually want to belong to God. But we cannot do it alone. The Holy Spirit, working through other members of the church, preaches the Word of God to us, teaches us in Sunday school, visits us in our homes, helps make up our minds, brings us to the house of worship, until we finally belong to God —or become sanctified.

We learn from this Bible verse that Christ died to make his church a body of holy people:

> ... as Christ loved the church and gave himself up for her, that he might sanctify her, having cleansed her by the washing of water with the word, that the church might be presented before him in splendor, without spot or wrinkle or any such thing, that she might be holy and without blemish.
> —Ephesians 5:25b-27

In this hymn we sing that God's holy church will last forever:

> *For not like kingdoms of the world*
> *Thy holy Church, O God,*
> *Though earthquake shocks are threatening her,*
> *And tempests are abroad;*
>
> *Unshaken as eternal hills,*
> *Immovable she stands,*
> *A mountain that shall fill the earth,*
> *A house not made with hands.*
> —154 SBH, 203 CSB

PRAYER

Dear Jesus, Lord of the church: I thank you for your church through which I have been brought to you. Amen. The Lord's Prayer.

Saturday *The Third Article*

"... and keeps it united with Jesus Christ in the one true faith."

God is always working to keep his church on the straight and narrow path of true religion. In the Old Testament we read that God spoke through his prophets who preached to the people, urging them to obey God's commandments and warning them not to worship false gods.

Often God had to emphasize his warnings by letting foreign enemies punish his people for their disobedience. When Christ came he preached against the church for obeying the law but forgetting to practice love. You remember that he had to drive the money-changers from the house of worship.

Martin Luther saw what bad things men were doing in the name of the church, and he finally had to break away from the old church and begin a new one. Through such men as the prophets and Luther, God has preserved his church and kept it pure and holy and close to him. God has promised that he will never forsake his church but that he will keep it forever.

Jesus promised that evil will not be able to win over his church:

> . . . and on this rock I will build my church, and the powers of death shall not prevail against it.
> —Matthew 16:18

In this hymn, based on Jesus' words, we sing about our belief that God's church will weather all the storms of life:

> *Built on a rock the church doth stand,*
> *Even when steeples are falling;*
> *Crumbled have spires in every land,*
> *Bells still are chiming and calling;*
> *Calling the young and old to rest,*
> *Calling the souls of men distressed,*
> *Longing for life everlasting.*
>
> —151 SBH

PRAYER

Dear Jesus, Lord of the church: I thank you for all those saints through whom you have preserved your church and kept it in the one true faith. Amen. The Lord's Prayer.

154

Sunday *The Third Article*

"... day after day he ... forgives ..."

Most of us would not think of saying to our friends, "Please, will you forgive me for everything bad that I am going to do for the next ten years?" How can we feel truly sorry and ask forgiveness for something we haven't even done yet? We need other people's forgiveness every day, because we are always doing things we should not, and not doing things we should do. We also need God's forgiveness every day. Every day we do and think and say things that are against his will. It is certainly true that Christ died once and for all in order that God might forgive our sins. But we must still ask for that forgiveness, and we must still feel sorry for our sins. And we must do it every day.

The Bible encourages us to come to God for forgiveness:

> If we confess our sins, he is faithful and just, and will forgive our sins and cleanse us from all unrighteousness.
> —1 John 1:9

In this hymn we ask God to forgive our sins of thought, word, and deed:

> To thee, O Lord, the God of all,
> With contrite heart I humbly call,
> And view my sins against thee, Lord,
> The sins of thought and deed and word;
> In my distress I cry to thee,
> O God, be merciful to me.
> —380 SBH

PRAYER

Dear heavenly Father: I thank you that you do daily forgive my sins. Help me to live each day more and more in keeping with your will. In Jesus' name. Amen. The Lord's Prayer.

". . . he fully forgives . . ."

Have you ever heard a person say, "I don't think I'll ever quite be able to forgive him for that!" The word "quite" implies that the person can forgive some of the wrong done to him, or even most of it, but not all of it. He cannot "fully" forgive. It may be that you yourself have this feeling toward someone. But God forgives fully, completely, holding nothing back. All he asks from us is that we be truly sorry and really want his forgiveness. Some churches teach that even though Christ died so that God would forgive our sins, yet we must earn that forgiveness by doing what is called "good works." Such teaching implies that Christ's death for us was not enough, and that we have to add something to what Christ did in order to be forgiven. Because God gave his only Son to die for our sins, we can be sure that our sins will be forgiven, if only we believe that Christ is our Savior. If we have such faith, as Luther says, our sins will be fully forgiven. We will have all the forgiveness we need. And we will then do good works out of thankfulness for what Christ has done for us.

The Bible tells us in many places that we are forgiven and saved by faith in what Christ has done for us and not by what we do:

> We ourselves . . . who know that a man is not justified by works of the law but through faith in Jesus Christ, even we have believed in Christ Jesus, in order to be justified by faith in Christ, and not by works of the law, because by works of the law shall no one be justified.
>
> —Galatians 2:15-16

In this hymn we say that we must depend entirely on God's love for our forgiveness:

> *With thee there is forgiveness, Lord,*
> *And love and grace abounding;*
> *The noblest thought and deed and word*
> *Were else but empty sounding.*
> *All guilty in thy sight appear;*
> *All to thy presence come in fear,*
> *And find thy lovingkindness.*
>
> —372 SBH

PRAYER

Dear heavenly Father: I thank you that you fully forgive all my sins. Help me to put all my trust in you. In Jesus' name. Amen. The Lord's Prayer.

Tuesday *The Third Article*

"... and the sins of all believers."

Christianity is a personal faith—that is, between each person and God. You must believe in God yourself—no one else can believe for you. And God can forgive you only if you yourself believe in him. He cannot forgive you because someone else believes.

But our Christian faith is not only between us and God—it is between us and other people also, especially other Christians. We can never live and act as though we are the only people who believe in God and whom God forgives. We must always remember that Christ died for all people and hope that they will come to God. That will make a big difference in the way we think and act toward others. For one thing, if Christ died for all men, because God made them and wants them to believe in him, then it is certainly wrong for us ever to think that we are better than anyone else. And for another thing, if we know that God forgives others, then we know that we ought to forgive them too—otherwise, how can we ask God to forgive us?

This passage of Scripture reminds us that we can't be selfish about our faith:

For God so loved the world that he gave his only Son, that whoever believes in him should not perish but have eternal life.

—John 3:16

In this hymn we express our desire for all people to be included in God's church:

O Spirit of the Lord, prepare
All the round earth her God to meet;
Breathe thou abroad like morning air,
Till hearts of stone begin to beat.

Baptize the nations; far and nigh
The triumphs of the Cross record;
The Name of Jesus glorify
Till every kindred call him Lord.

—306 SBH

PRAYER

Dear heavenly Father: Help me to forgive others with the same love with which you have forgiven me. Amen. The Lord's Prayer.

"... on the last day ..."

As far back as anyone can remember and as far back as there are historical records, the physical world has been as it is today. Summer, fall, winter, and spring always come and go. The sun always rises in the morning and sets in the evening. The stars are always there, and each spring new leaves and grass and flowers appear. It is easy to believe that things will always continue that way. It is easy to believe that people will always be born and grow old and die. But the Bible tells us that there will be a "last day" for us and for our world—that things will not go on forever. When Christ comes again, life and the world as we know it will pass away, and there will be a new life and a new world. Scientists and the Bible tell us that our world was not always here, and the Bible tells us that there is a time coming when it will not be here. As Christians we should live as though that "last day" were coming tomorrow. No one knows!

The Bible plainly teaches an end to our world:

> But the day of the Lord will come like a thief, and then the heavens will pass away with a loud noise, and the elements will be dissolved with fire, and the earth and the works that are upon it will be burned up. But according to his promise we wait for new heavens and a new earth in which righteousness dwells.
>
> —2 Peter 3:10 and 13

We sing in this hymn of our trust in God, no matter what may come:

> *I know not what the future hath*
> *Of marvel or surprise,*
> *Assured alone that life and death*
> *His mercy underlies.*
>
> *And so beside the silent sea*
> *I wait the muffled oar;*
> *No harm from him can come to me*
> *On ocean or on shore.*
>
> —593 SBH

PRAYER

Dear heavenly Father: Help me to trust in you and not to fear the future. In Jesus' name. Amen. The Lord's Prayer.

Thursday   *The Third Article*

"... he will raise me ..."

Our Lord promises that if we believe in him, we will be raised from the dead, just as he was, and will live forever. Jews and Christians are the only people who believe in such a raising-up, or resurrection. Many people, as St. Paul says in the New Testament, think that such a belief is foolishness. Even if a dead body could be brought back to life, such people ask, what about those whose bodies have been buried so long they are only dust, or those that have been bombed or burned? How can such bodies be "raised" again? As Christians we believe that the same God who made our bodies the first time out of the elements of the air and the soil, can give us new bodies, either from those same elements, or from others. When our bodies decay, they simply go back into the air and the soil from which they came, just like a log burning in the fireplace. The elements out of which our bodies were made are not lost, but simply change their form. Why then is it so foolish to believe that God can take such elements and put them together again in a different way so that we will have bodies that will last forever?

Jesus himself promises us that he will give life to us again after death:

> For this is the will of my Father, that every one who sees the Son and believes in him should have eternal life; and I will raise him up at the last day.
>
> —John 6:40

The double theme of our Easter hymns is that because Jesus rose from the dead, we too shall be raised:

> *As thou didst rise on Easter Day,*
> *Help us to rise from sin, we pray;*
> *And at the end of earthly strife*
> *Raise us, O Lord, to endless life.*
>
> —102 SBH

PRAYER

Dear heavenly Father: I thank you for your promise of a new life with you in the world to come. Amen. The Lord's Prayer.

"... and all the dead ..."

People who do not believe in the resurrection of the body believe that death is the end of everything. They do not believe that our souls will live forever in new bodies. There are some Christians who think that only those who believe in Christ will rise again. But the Bible teaches that all people, bad as well as good, and non-Christians as well as Christians, will be raised from the dead when Christ comes again. The Bible teaches that death is not the end for anyone, but that all people who have ever lived will have to stand before the throne of God. If more people knew this and believed it, they would certainly live different lives. What a wonderful place this world would be if everyone believed that there is a life after death and that we do not have to answer to ourselves alone, but that a day is coming when everyone will have to answer to God.

St. Paul speaks to all people in these verses:

> ... For we shall all stand before the judgment seat of God; for it is written, "As I live, says the Lord, every knee shall bow to me, and every tongue shall give praise to God." So each of us shall give account of himself to God.
>
> —Romans 14:10b-12

This hymn says that we will all some day stand before God on Judgment Day:

> *When his servants stand before him*
>   *Each receiving his reward,*
> *When his saints in light adore him,*
>   *Giving glory to the Lord;*
> *"Victory!" our song shall be*
> *Like the thunder of the sea.*
>
> —556 SBH, 472 LH, 202 CSB

PRAYER

Dear heavenly Father: Help me to live in such a way in this life that I will have nothing to fear in the next. In Jesus' name. Amen. The Lord's Prayer.

160

Saturday   *The Third Article*

". . . and give me and all believers in Christ eternal life."

According to our Christian faith, there are two kinds of everlasting life. The Bible calls one heaven and the other hell. Heaven is the place where those who love and obey God in this life will live with him forever in the life after death. Hell is the place where those who do not love and obey God will live apart from him in eternity, because they do not want to be with him. We can see in this life that people who hate and disobey God can make a "hell on earth" by their cruelty and wickedness and the suffering they cause. We can also see in examples of Christian love and kindness and happiness how wonderful it will be to live forever with God and do his will.

Jesus tells us in plain language about the two kinds of eternal life:

> Then the King will say to those at his right hand, 'Come, O blessed of my Father, inherit the kingdom prepared for you from the foundation of the world'; . . . Then he will say to those at his left hand, 'Depart from me, you cursed, into the eternal fire prepared for the devil and his angels'; . . . And they will go away into eternal punishment, but the righteous into eternal life.
>
> —Matthew 25:34, 41, 46

In many of our hymns we sing about the beauties and joys of everlasting life with God:

> *There's a home for little children*
> *Above the bright blue sky,*
> *Where Jesus reigns in glory,*
> *A home of peace and joy;*
> *No home on earth is like it,*
> *Nor can with it compare;*
> *For every one is happy,*
> *Nor could be happier there.*
>
> —592 SBH

PRAYER

Dear heavenly Father: Help me to love and obey you in this life so that I may be with you forever in the next. In Jesus' name. Amen. The Lord's Prayer.

PART THREE

The Lord's Prayer

THE INTRODUCTION

Our Father who art in heaven.

*What does
this mean?*

Here God encourages us to believe
that he is truly our Father
and we are his children.

We therefore are to pray to him with
complete confidence
just as children speak to their loving
father.

THE FIRST PETITION

Hallowed be thy name.

*What does
this mean?*

God's name certainly is holy in itself,
but we ask in this prayer
that we may keep it holy.

*When does
this happen?*

God's name is hallowed
whenever his Word is rightly taught
and we as children of God live in
harmony with it.
Help us to do this, heavenly Father!

But anyone who teaches or lives contrary
to the Word of God
dishonors God's name among us.
Keep us from doing this, heavenly
Father!

THE SECOND PETITION

Thy kingdom come.

What does this mean?

God's kingdom comes indeed
without our praying for it,
but we ask in this prayer that it
may come also to us.

When does this happen?

God's kingdom comes
when our heavenly Father gives us his
Holy Spirit,
so that by his grace we believe his
holy Word
and live a godly life on earth now
and in heaven forever.

THE THIRD PETITION

Thy will be done on earth as it is in heaven.

What does this mean?

The good and gracious will of God is
surely done without our prayer,
but we ask in this prayer
that it may be done also among us.

When does this happen?

God's will is done when he hinders and
defeats every evil scheme and purpose
of the devil, the world, and our sinful
self,
which would prevent us from keeping
his name holy
and would oppose the coming of his
kingdom.
And his will is done
when he strengthens our faith
and keeps us firm in his Word as long as
we live.

THE FOURTH PETITION

Give us this day our daily bread.

What does this mean?

God gives daily bread, even without
    our prayer, to all people though sinful,
but we ask in this prayer
that he will help us to realize this
and to receive our daily bread with
    thanks.

What is meant by "daily bread"?

Daily bread includes everything needed
    for this life,
such as food and clothing, home and
    property,
work and income, a devoted family,
an orderly community, good govern-
    ment,
favorable weather, peace and health,
a good name, and true friends and
    neighbors.

THE FIFTH PETITION

*And forgive us our trespasses, as we forgive those who
trespass against us.*

What does this mean?

We ask in this prayer
that our Father in heaven would not
    hold our sins against us
and because of them refuse to hear our
    prayer.

And we pray that he would give us
    everything by grace,
for we sin every day
and deserve nothing but punishment.

So we on our part will heartily forgive
and gladly do good to those who sin
    against us.

164

THE SIXTH PETITION

And lead us not into temptation.

What does this mean?

God tempts no one to sin,
but we ask in this prayer that God would
   watch over us
so that the devil, the world, and our
   sinful self may not deceive us
and draw us into unbelief, despair,
   and other great and shameful sins.

And we pray that even though we are
   so tempted
we may still win the final victory.

THE SEVENTH PETITION

But deliver us from evil.

What does this mean?

We ask in this inclusive prayer
that our heavenly Father would save us
   from every evil to body and soul,
and at our last hour would mercifully
   take us
from the troubles of this world to himself
   in heaven.

THE DOXOLOGY

For thine is the kingdom and the power and the glory forever and ever. Amen.

What does "Amen" mean?

Amen means *Yes, it shall be so.*
We say *Amen* because we are certain
that such petitions are pleasing to
   our Father in heaven.
For he himself has commanded us to
   pray in this way
and has promised to hear us.

165

"Our Father who art in heaven."

If God had simply made us and then left us alone, we could still call him Creator, but not Father. But God did not leave us to ourselves. The Book of Genesis tells us that God made the whole world and everything in it so that man could live and have food and companionship and enjoy life. The Bible tells us that God walked and talked with Adam and Eve, and took care of their every need. That is why we can and should call God our Father. God talks to us in prayer, and he takes care of our every need, if we put our trust in him and obey his Word. When we are happy, God is happy for us; and when we are in pain or sorrow, God feels it as if it were his own. Nothing that happens in our lives is too small for him to notice or too big for him to help us overcome.

Jesus tells us how much our heavenly Father cares for us:

> Are not two sparrows sold for a penny? And not one of them will fall to the ground without your Father's will. But even the hairs of your head are all numbered. Fear not, therefore; you are of more value than many sparrows.
> —Matthew 10:29-31

This hymn also tells about God's fatherly care for us:

> *Father-like he tends and spares us,*
> *Well our feeble frame he knows;*
> *In his hands he gently bears us,*
> *Rescues us from all our foes:*
> *Alleluia! Alleluia!*
> *Widely as his mercy flows.*
> —160 SBH, 289 CSB

PRAYER

O God, our heavenly Father: I thank you that you watch over me and provide me with all that I need. In Jesus' name. Amen. The Lord's Prayer.

166

The Introduction

"Here God encourages us to believe that he is truly our Father . . ."

God encourages us to call him our Father. Because we are human, we must think in human pictures and speak in human language. Everyone has a picture of an ideal father in his mind, and everyone knows what is meant when he hears the word "father." God wants us to think of him as the ideal Father, who is loving and kind, but who still demands that we do what is right; who protects us from harm and danger; who is wise, strong, forgiving; who is more ready to give than we are to ask. Jesus always talked about God as not only his Father, but as the Father of all who believe in him. That is why we have the Lord's Prayer: Jesus told his disciples to pray, "Our Father, who art in heaven. . ." Whatever our earthly fathers may be like, or whatever may happen to them, we know that we will never be without a Father, because we will always have one in heaven.

God tells us that he wants to be our Father:

> Therefore come out from them,
> and be separate from them, says the Lord,
> and touch nothing unclean;
> then I will welcome you,
> and I will be a father to you,
> and you shall be my sons and daughters,
> says the Lord Almighty.
>
> —2 Corinthians 6:17-18

In this hymn we sing about God's care for us, his children:

> *Children of the heavenly Father*
> *Safely in his bosom gather;*
> *Nestling bird nor star in heaven*
> *Such a refuge e'er was given.*
>
> —572 SBH

PRAYER

O God, our heavenly Father: Help me to feel your love for me so that I will want to be close to you and pray to you often. In Jesus' name. Amen. The Lord's Prayer.

Tuesday   *The Introduction*

". . . and we are his children."

We have said that we should think of God as our Father. If we do that, then we can and should think of ourselves as his children. People who do not believe there is a God and that they are his children, often become heartless and evil and do terrible things to each other. If we think of ourselves as God's children, we will live accordingly. We will try to say and do the things that please our heavenly Father. We will not be afraid, because we know that we have a heavenly Father who watches over us and leads and guides us through life. And we will treat others with love and consideration because we know that God loves all his children and wants them to live as brothers and sisters.

The Bible tells us that there is nothing more wonderful than to be a child of God:

> When we cry, "Abba! Father!" it is the Spirit himself bearing witness with our spirit that we are children of God, and if children, then heirs, heirs of God and fellow heirs with Christ. . . .
>
> —Romans 8:15b-17a

This hymn reminds us of God's love for us, his children:

> *Neither life nor death shall ever*
> *From the Lord his children sever;*
> *Unto them his grace he showeth,*
> *And their sorrows all he knoweth.*
>
> *Though he giveth or he taketh,*
> *God his children ne'er forsaketh,*
> *His the loving purpose solely*
> *To preserve them pure and holy.*
>
> —572 SBH

PRAYER

O God, our heavenly Father: May I never forget that I am your child and that my life should be pleasing to you. In Jesus' name. Amen. The Lord's Prayer.

"We therefore are to pray to him with complete confidence . . ."

When we do something with confidence, we are sure of it. We may be sure that when we call upon God he will hear us because he is our Father. There are those who feel that God is too busy to be bothered with all our problems and troubles and wants, or that he is so far above us that he is not interested. But God wants and asks us to call on him with all confidence. He wants us to be sure that because he is our Father and we are his children, we can come to him with anything that would make a child want to come to its father. It is through prayer that we can call upon God, and it is through prayer that he answers us. Just as we need to talk to our earthly father in order to know him and learn to have confidence in him, so we have to pray regularly and often in order to learn to love and trust our heavenly Father.

St. John talks about the confidence we can have in God:

> And this is the confidence which we have in him, that if we ask anything according to his will he hears us. And if we know that he hears us in whatever we ask, we know that we have obtained the requests made of him.
>
> —1 John 5:14-15

We express our confidence in God in this hymn:

> *The King of love my shepherd is,*
> *Whose goodness faileth never;*
> *I nothing lack if I am his,*
> *And he is mine for ever.*
> —530 SBH, 431 LH, 345 CSB

PRAYER

O God, our heavenly Father: I thank you that I can have perfect confidence and trust in you for all my needs. In Jesus' name. Amen. The Lord's Prayer.

". . . just as children speak to their loving father."

A child who needs something speaks to his parents about it because he is confident (that is, he is certain) that his parents will do something about it. And we can be just as confident that when we speak to our heavenly Father about our needs, he will do something about them. He cannot always do just what we ask. Just as earthly parents have to use their judgment about how to help their children, so God must often help us in ways we do not understand, or which we may not understand until years later. He knows us better than we know ourselves, and he knows that many of the things we ask for would harm rather than help us. But we can always have complete confidence that our heavenly Father hears our prayers and that he will do something about them that will be for our good.

Jesus encourages us to come to God with our needs:

> Truly, truly, I say to you, if you ask anything of the Father, he will give it to you in my name. Hitherto you have asked nothing in my name; ask, and you will receive, that your joy may be full.
>
> —John 16:23-24

One of our most comforting hymns invites us to come to God in prayer:

What a friend we have in Jesus,
  All our sins and griefs to bear!
What a privilege to carry
  Everything to God in prayer!
O what peace we often forfeit,
  O what needless pain we bear,
All because we do not carry
  Everything to God in prayer!

Have we trials and temptations?
  Is there trouble anywhere?
We should never be discouraged;
  Take it to the Lord in prayer.
Can we find a friend so faithful,
  Who will all our sorrows share?
Jesus knows our every weakness;
  Take it to the Lord in prayer.

—459 SBH, 457 LH

PRAYER

Dear heavenly Father: Help me to come to you in complete confidence that my prayers will be answered according to your will. In Jesus' name. Amen. The Lord's Prayer.

       The First Petition

"God's name ... is holy in itself ..."

There have been many false gods in whom people have believed and still do, and they have strange names, depending on the country in which they are worshiped. But there is only one true God, only one real God, who is not an idol made by men or thought up in men's minds. We did not make him—he made us and everything that exists. So the name "God" applies to him alone, and his name is hallowed, or holy.

St. Paul tells us why the name of God is holy:

> The God who made the world and everything in it, being Lord of heaven and earth, does not live in shrines made by man, nor is he served by human hands, as though he needed anything, since he himself gives to all men life and breath and everything. . . . Being then God's offspring, we ought not to think that the Deity is like gold, or silver, or stone, a representation by the art and imagination of man.
> —Acts 17:24-25 and 29

In this hymn we sing that there is only one holy God:

> *Holy, holy, holy! though the darkness hide thee,*
> *Though the eye of sinful man thy glory may not see,*
> *Only thou art holy; there is none beside thee,*
> *Perfect in power, in love, and purity.*
> —131 SBH, 246 LH, 158 CSB

PRAYER

O God, our heavenly Father: I praise you for your power and glory and holiness, and for all the wonderful things you have done. In Jesus' name. Amen. The Lord's Prayer.

        The First Petition

"... but we ask in this prayer that we may keep it holy."

There is always danger in having freedom. The danger is that we may use our freedom to do nothing, or to do what is wrong. Generally speaking, we Lutherans have very few rules and regulations that we must follow in our churches. Things are left pretty much to our own consciences. No one threatens us or makes us do what we don't want to do. But we often abuse our freedom. We do not always use our freedom to hallow God's name and keep it holy by attending church and Sunday school regularly, by having devotions at home, and by our life and conversation. Just because no one makes us do these things, we have to make an extra effort to do them on our own.

St. Peter tells us how we can best keep God's name holy:

> ... but as he who called you is holy, be holy yourselves in all your conduct; since it is written, "You shall be holy, for I am holy."
>
>   —1 Peter 1:15-16

In this hymn we confess that God's name is holy to us:

> *O Saviour, precious Saviour,*
> *Whom yet unseen we love;*
> *O Name of might and favor,*
> *All other names above;*
> *We worship thee, we bless thee,*
> *To thee alone we sing;*
> *We praise thee and confess thee,*
> *Our holy Lord and King.*
>   —419 SBH, 352 LH, 361 CSB

PRAYER

O God, our heavenly Father: Help me always to keep your name holy in my own heart and mind and speech. In Jesus' name. Amen. The Lord's Prayer.

Sunday   *The Second Petition*

"Thy kingdom come."

No thoughtful Christian can be happy with the world the way it is. The minute we look around and see how things really are, then we can no longer be satisfied. How can a Christian be satisfied when two-thirds of the people of the world do not have enough to eat and wear; when there is crime and greed everywhere, even in the highest government offices; when the nations of the world still settle their differences with terrible weapons of war; when so often the innocent suffer and the guilty go unpunished? The only true satisfaction we Christians have is knowing that when God's kingdom comes, all wrongs will be made right, and we will live with God and one another in love and peace. That is why we ought to pray every day, "Thy Kingdom come!"

A beautiful vision of God's kingdom is described in Revelation:

> Then I saw a new heaven and a new earth; for the first heaven and the first earth had passed away, and the sea was no more. And I saw the holy city, new Jerusalem, coming down out of heaven from God, prepared as a bride adorned for her husband; and I heard a great voice from the throne saying, "Behold, the dwelling of God is with men. He will dwell with them, and they shall be his people, and God himself will be with them; he will wipe away every tear from their eyes, and death shall be no more, neither shall there be mourning nor crying nor pain anymore, for the former things have passed away."   —Revelation 21:1-4

This same desire for God's kingdom to come is expressed in the following hymn:

> *Jerusalem, thou city fair and high,*
>   *Would God I were in thee!*
> *My longing heart fain, fain to thee would fly!*
>   *It will not stay with me;*
> *Far over vale and mountain,*
>   *Far over field and plain,*
> *It hastes to seek its fountain*
>   *And quit this world of pain.*
>   —588 SBH, 619 LH

PRAYER

Dear heavenly Father: May your kingdom come soon, when peace and love and happiness shall reign. Amen. The Lord's Prayer.

Monday   *The Second Petition*

"God's kingdom comes indeed . . ."

It is a wonderful thing for us to know that the God in whom we believe is all-powerful; that there is nothing he cannot do; that he is the Maker of heaven and earth. We know that when he makes a promise he will keep it; there is nothing that can stop him. So we know that God's kingdom is coming, because he promised that it will, no matter how the devil and his followers try to stop it, no matter how hopeless the world situation looks. Many people do not believe that the kingdom of God is coming. They say that people thought it was coming at different times in history, but it has not come and never will. But we must remember that to God a day is like a thousand years and a thousand years is like a day. We had better believe God and be ready. This life is all the time we have to get ready, and we never know when it will end.

In this parable in which the "master of the house" is really God, Jesus warns us to be ready for the kingdom when it comes:

> Watch therefore—for you do not know when the master of the house will come, in the evening or at midnight, or at cockcrow, or in the morning—lest he come suddenly and find you asleep. And what I say to you I say to all: Watch.
> —Mark 13:35-37

The same idea of watching for the kingdom is in the words of this favorite hymn of the Advent season, just before Christmas:

Rejoice, all ye believers,
   And let your lights appear;
The evening is advancing
   And darker night is near;
The Bridegroom is arising,
   And soon he draweth nigh;
Up, pray, and watch, and wrestle,
   At midnight comes the cry!

The watchers on the mountain
   Proclaim the Bridegroom near;
Go meet him as he cometh
   With hallelujahs clear;
The marriage-feast is waiting,
   The gates wide open stand;
Up, up ye heirs of glory,
   The Bridegroom is at hand!
   —14 SBH, 13 CSB

PRAYER

Dear heavenly Father: Help me to have a strong faith and to live in such a way that I will be ready for your kingdom to come at any time. In Jesus' name. Amen. The Lord's Prayer.

"... without our praying for it ..."

It is hard for us to believe that God's kingdom will come, whether we do anything to help it come or not. It makes us feel more important to believe that we are partners with God in bringing his kingdom to earth, and that unless we do our part, it might never come. But that is not at all what the Bible teaches. The New Testament tells us that God is going to make this earth of ours disappear altogether and that a new earth will take its place. It is on this new earth that God's kingdom will be. We can no more help to make a new earth than we could help to make this one. God must do it all. But we can and should pray that we will be ready to live in it when it comes; and we should always be praying for others and helping them to prepare for it too.

Hundreds of years before the birth of Christ, the prophet Isaiah said that God would bring his kingdom into being:

> Of the increase of his government and of peace
>> there will be no end,
> upon the throne of David, and over his kingdom,
>> to establish it, and to uphold it
> with justice and with righteousness
>> from this time forth and for evermore.
> The zeal of the Lord of hosts will do this.
>
> —Isaiah 9:7

When we sing this hymn we say that we know for sure that God's kingdom will come:

> *His kingdom cannot fail,*
> *He rules o'er earth and heaven,*
> *The keys of death and hell*
> *Are to our Jesus given:*
>
> *He sits at God's right hand*
> *Till all his foes submit,*
> *And bow to his command,*
> *And fall beneath his feet.*
>
> —436 SBH, 126 CSB

PRAYER

Dear heavenly Father: Hear my prayer that all people will want to live in your kingdom when it comes. In Jesus' name. Amen. The Lord's Prayer.

". . . but we ask in this prayer that it may come also to us."

It is true that the kingdom of God will come without our prayers or actions. But it is not going to come to *us* without our prayers and actions! Jesus says many times in the New Testament that the most awful thing that can happen to us is to be left out of the kingdom. He tells about people who were not ready for the kingdom and who were thrown into "the outer darkness; there men will weep and gnash their teeth." By praying to God that his kingdom may come, we show him that we love him and want to live with him forever as his obedient children. Then God knows that we truly want him to be our Father and want to be a part of his kingdom. We can be sure that he will hear these prayers and answer them.

St. Paul was sure that because he loved God and prayed to him, he would be in his kingdom, along with all others who loved God:

> I have fought the good fight, I have finished the race, I have kept the faith. Henceforth there is laid up for me the crown of righteousness, which the Lord, the righteous judge, will award to me on that Day, and not only to me but also to all who have loved his appearing.
>
> —2 Timothy 4:7-8

In this famous Advent hymn we ask God that his kingdom would come to us:

> *O come, thou Rod of Jesse, free*
> *Thine own from Satan's tyranny;*
> *From depths of hell thy people save,*
> *And give them victory o'er the grave.*
> *Rejoice, rejoice! Emmanuel*
> *Shall come to thee, O Israel.*
>
> —2 SBH, 1 CSB

PRAYER

Dear heavenly Father: I pray that when your kingdom comes, it will come to me also, and that I will be your child forever. In Jesus' name. Amen. The Lord's Prayer.

Thursday   *The Second Petition*

". . . when our heavenly Father gives us his Holy Spirit . . ."

Even though God's kingdom will come to a new earth, at some time in the future, there is a way in which it comes to us now, even while we are on this earth. God's kingdom comes to us in spirit—his Holy Spirit. It is not simply a matter of being here in the world one day and in God's kingdom the next day. We have to be made ready. It takes much preparation to move from one home to another in this life. You can't expect to feel at home in God's kingdom until his Spirit changes your sinful nature, or until he makes you over into a new sort of person who will want to be with God forever. When the Spirit does that, then you are already a member of God's spiritual kingdom, here and now.

Jesus said that his kingdom could be in people's hearts, even in this life:

> The kingdom of God is not coming with signs to be observed; nor will they say, "Lo, here it is!" or "There!" for behold, the kingdom of God is in the midst of you.
> —Luke 17:20-21

We ask Jesus in this hymn to change our lives by the power of his Holy Spirit:

Before the dawning day
Let sin's dark deeds be gone;
The old man all be put away,
The new man all put on.

All glory to the Son,
Who comes to set us free,
With Father, Spirit, ever One,
Through all eternity.

—3 SBH, 4 CSB

PRAYER

Dear heavenly Father: Help me to have your kingdom in my heart. In Jesus' name. Amen. The Lord's Prayer.

Friday   *The Second Petition*

"... so that by his grace we believe his holy word ..."

The first thing that the Holy Spirit has to do to get us ready for God's kingdom is to enlighten our minds so that we will believe God's Word when we read it and hear it preached. Until we come to believe God's Word there is no hope for us, because only this Word can show us the way to God's kingdom. That is why God's Word is called his revelation. It reveals, or shows us, something that is otherwise hidden from us. If we look around us, we can see people heading for destruction because they do not believe in God's Word. We read daily in the headlines of our newspapers about all the evil things people do which lead toward hell. The world could not go on at all, even for another year, if it were not for those who do believe in God's Word and who have his kingdom in their hearts.

St. John tells us that the Bible was written so that we can believe God's Word and be saved for his kingdom:

> ... but these are written that you may believe that Jesus is the Christ, the Son of God, and that believing you may have life in his name.
>
> —John 20:31

This hymn says that God's Word will guide us through life and bring us at last to his kingdom:

> *Through sorrow's night my sun shall be*
> *God's word—a treasure dear to me,*
> *My shield and buckler ever.*
> *My title as his child and heir*
> *The Father's hand hath written there,*
> *His promise failing never:*
> *"Thou shalt be mine forever."*
>
> —253 SBH, 48 LH

PRAYER

Dear heavenly Father: Help me to believe your Holy Word and to make it my guide for life, so that I may enter into your kingdom. In Jesus' name. Amen. The Lord's Prayer.

Saturday *The Second Petition*

"... and live a godly life on earth now and in heaven forever."

The Holy Spirit must do something more than enlighten our minds to make us ready for God's kingdom. He must give us the courage and strength to live a Christian life. We cannot prepare for eternal life with our heavenly Father by leading wicked, sinful lives now. We will never be perfect in this life, it is true; but all of us can come much closer to the kind of life God wants us to live. We have to remember too that we do not live only to ourselves. Others see our actions and hear our words. It is through us that others must be won for God's kingdom, and we can never do our job as missionaries by leading a life that is a bad example for others. We must show by our actions that we are members of the kingdom of God.

Jesus himself tells us that it is our responsibility to lead lives that are good examples to others:

Let your light so shine before men, that they may see your good works and give glory to your Father who is in heaven.
—Matthew 5:16

We ask Jesus in this hymn to help us lead a godly life:

O Jesus, I have promised
To serve thee to the end;
Be thou forever near me.
My master and my friend;
I shall not fear the battle
If thou art by my side,
Nor wander from the pathway
If thou wilt be my guide.

O Jesus, thou hast promised
To all who follow thee,
That where thou art in glory
There shall thy servant be;
And, Jesus, I have promised
To serve thee to the end;
O give me grace to follow,
My master and my friend.
—515 SBH

PRAYER

Dear heavenly Father: Give me strength to overcome the temptation to do what is wrong, so that I can live a life that pleases you and that helps others. In Jesus' name. Amen. The Lord's Prayer.

"Thy will be done . . ."

When we say that a person wills something, we mean that he wants something. Whatever a person wills is what he wants. When a man makes out his will before he dies, he puts down on paper what he wants done with his property after he is gone. God, too, has a will. There are things he wants. The trouble is that most people live as though God did not have a will, as though there weren't anything he wanted, as though he had no plans. But God does have a will; he does have plans; and he has them for you and me. He wants us to live in peace and love with one another and to get ourselves ready for his everlasting kingdom, which he has promised us will come. God has told us about his will in the Bible, and he wants us to know about it and to live according to it. Then the will of God will be done, at least in our lives.

The Apostle Paul warns us that we ought to know God's will:

> Therefore do not be foolish, but understand what the will of the Lord is.
> —Ephesians 5:17

In this hymn we ask for help to want God's will done in our lives:

> *My God and Father, while I stray*
> *Far from my home in life's rough way,*
> *O teach me from my heart to say,*
> *"Thy will be done."*
>
> *Renew my will from day to day,*
> *Blend it with thine, and take away*
> *All that now makes it hard to say,*
> *"Thy will be done."*
> —465 SBH, 418 LH, 408 CSB

PRAYER

Dear heavenly Father: Help me always to be mindful of your will and to live my life according to it. In Jesus' name. Amen. The Lord's Prayer.

"... on earth ..."

Sometimes it is hard for us to understand why God's will is not done on earth more than it is. Every time we read or hear of a crime, or we have a fight with our brother or sister, God's will is not being done. God's will is so good and perfect that if everyone obeyed it, the world would be a wonderful place to live, because there would be no more suffering or crime or sorrow. What we forget is that in order to do God's will all the time, we would all have to change. Governments would have to change, businesses would have to change, the way everyone lives most of the time would have to change. Everybody and everything would have to change and become good and truthful and full of love. But the devil works on us so that we want to keep our old ways and not let God change us. So God's will is not done on earth as much as it ought to be, but it should be done most of all by those of us who say we believe in God and love him.

We learn from the New Testament that Christians are supposed to lead the way in doing God's will on earth:

> Do not be conformed to this world but be transformed by the renewal of your mind, that you may prove what is the will of God, what is good and acceptable and perfect.
> —Romans 12:2

In this hymn we ask Jesus to guide us and keep us in God's will:

> O Master, let me walk with thee
> In lowly paths of service free;
> Tell me thy secret; help me bear
> The strain of toil, the fret of care.
>
> Help me the slow of heart to move
> By some clear, winning word of love;
> Teach me the wayward feet to stay,
> And guide them in the homeward way.
> —537 SBH

PRAYER

Dear heavenly Father: I pray that your will may be done on earth through my own life. In Jesus' name. Amen. The Lord's Prayer.

181

Tuesday   *The Third Petition*

". . . as it is in heaven."

We don't know too much about what heaven is like, but we can be sure of one thing: It is a place—the only place—where God's will is always done in everything. As was pointed out in yesterday's devotion, here on earth God's will is done only some of the time by some of the people. In those places on earth where God's will is done more often than usual, there a bit of heaven exists from time to time, as people actually put love and forgiveness and helpfulness into practice. But even if God's will can never be done on the whole earth as it is in heaven, we should always pray that through those of us who believe in Jesus, God's will may be done in whatever corner of the world we live: in our homes, in our schools, at our work, in our neighborhoods. God's will never fails. It is always being done somewhere. We pray that it may be done where we are.

We Christians are reminded in the New Testament that heaven is always to be our guide and goal for our thoughts, words, and deeds here on earth:

> But our commonwealth is in heaven, and from it we await
> a Savior, the Lord Jesus Christ.
> —Philippians 3:20

Of all our national hymns, this one expresses most clearly our desire to have God's will done in our country as it is in heaven:

> *O beautiful for spacious skies,*
> *For amber waves of grain,*
> *For purple mountain majesties*
> *Above the fruited plain!*
> *America! America!*
> *God shed his grace on thee,*
> *And crown thy good with brotherhood*
> *From sea to shining sea.*
> —346 SBH

PRAYER

Dear heavenly Father: I pray that your will may be done in my home, in my neighborhood, in my country, and throughout the whole world, as it is in heaven. In Jesus' name. Amen. The Lord's Prayer.

Wednesday   *The Third Petition*

". . . but we ask in this prayer that it may be done also among us."

It is easy to become discouraged when we try to do God's will in a world where so many others are doing just the opposite. We may think, "What's the use of trying? I'm only one person against so many!" Whenever we feel like that, it will help us to remember that God's will has often had to be carried out by only one person or a small group. Jesus himself had to start all alone and against very powerful enemies. His command to go "into all the world" to spread his teachings was given to only a handful of disciples. Paul had to work almost single-handedly to carry the message of Jesus to the countries of the Mediterranean Sea, outside Palestine. And the founder of our church, Martin Luther, had to stand alone many times for what he believed was God's will. We can also find strength in being members of the church, in having worship and fellowship with others who are also trying to do God's will.

St. Paul gives us encouragement from his own personal experience in doing God's will:

> And let us not grow weary in well-doing, for in due season we shall reap, if we do not lose heart.
> —Galatians 6:9

This hymn gives comfort and courage to the people of God who are trying to do his will:

> *Fear not, thou faithful Christian flock;*
> *God is thy shelter and thy rock;*
> *Fear not for thy salvation.*
> *Though fierce the foe and dark the night,*
> *The Lord of hosts shall be thy might,*
> *Christ thine illumination.*
> —156 SBH

PRAYER

Dear heavenly Father: May the example of the heroes of our faith and the fellowship of the church give me strength to do your will. In Jesus' name, Amen. The Lord's Prayer.

183

"God's will is done when he hinders and defeats every evil scheme and purpose of the devil . . ."

God's will is not the only one that is at work in the world. There is another will which is always against God's, and which is always trying to lead people to disobey God's will. That is the devil's will. That is how it is possible for us actually to enjoy sinning. The devil takes over our will and makes it his. From then on we want what he wants, and what he wants is never what God wants. When the devil's will controls us, we want to do and say and think those things which we know are against God's commands and which bring only trouble and sorrow and pain for us and others. The only way to keep the devil from controlling our wills is to let God control them. Where he is, the devil cannot come. There is not room enough for the devil's will and God's will at the same time.

St. James gives us good advice on how to win our battles with the devil:

> Submit yourselves therefore to God. Resist the devil and he will flee from you.
>
> —James 4:7

The devil was very real to Martin Luther. In this hymn Luther says that through God and his Word we can win over the devil:

> *And though this world, with devils filled,*
> *Should threaten to undo us;*
> *We will not fear, for God hath willed*
> *His truth to triumph through us:*
> *The prince of darkness grim,*
> *We tremble not for him;*
> *His rage we can endure,*
> *For lo! his doom is sure,*
> *One little word shall fell him.*
>
> —150 SBH

PRAYER

Dear heavenly Father: Keep me in your will and protect me from the will of the devil. In Jesus' name. Amen. The Lord's Prayer.

184

Friday *The Third Petition*

"... when he hinders and defeats every evil scheme and purpose of ... the world ..."

The world cannot have a scheme and purpose of its own, but the devil works out his purpose through the world. He makes the things of the world so attractive to us that we want them more than anything else and will do anything to get them. Because we who live in twentieth century America are flooded with so many things and encouraged by advertisements to buy more and more of them, our greatest danger as Christians is that we will devote all our time and energy and money—our whole life—to getting houses, cars, automatic washers, hi-fi sets, television sets, fashionable clothes, and model railway trains. Then we will forget about God and his kingdom and his will for us, and that is exactly what the devil wants. We should remember that even our Lord was tempted by the devil, who showed him all the kingdoms of the world and their riches and promised to give them to Jesus if Jesus would worship him. We must always be on guard that the devil does not get us to worship him through the things of the world.

The best advice on this subject is given us by Jesus himself:

> Therefore do not be anxious, saying, "What shall we eat?" or "What shall we drink?" or "What shall we wear?" For the Gentiles seek all these things; and your heavenly Father knows that you need them all. But seek first his kingdom and his righteousness, and all these things shall be yours as well.
> —Matthew 6:31-33

In one of our most wonderful hymns we say that we love Jesus above all our earthly possessions:

> *When I survey the wondrous Cross*
> *On which the Prince of Glory died,*
> *My richest gain I count but loss*
> *And pour contempt on all my pride.*
> —503 SBH, 175 LH, 97 CSB

PRAYER

Dear heavenly Father: Give me enough faith to believe that if I put you and your will first in my life, the worldly things that I need will be taken care of. In Jesus' name. Amen. The Lord's Prayer.

Saturday   *The Third Petition*

". . . when he hinders and defeats every evil scheme and purpose of . . . our sinful self . . ."

It is through our own bodies and minds and senses that the devil can make the things of the world look so tempting to us. That is how Eve was tempted to eat the fruit of the tree that God had forbidden her and Adam to taste. The devil made the fruit look so delicious to her through her sense of sight—and, through her mind he made her imagine how good it would taste—that she could not resist. The devil works the same way today. Hospitals are full of people who simply cannot control their appetites, their desire to eat and drink and smoke too much. Jails are full of people who have let the devil tempt them through their minds into planning and carrying out all sorts of crimes. Because we are spiritually weak and sinful, and liable to fall into temptation, we should pray daily that God will give us the strength to discipline our minds and bodies and senses so that they do his will and not the devil's.

The Apostle Paul tells us how wrong it is to give in to the evil desires of our minds and bodies:

> For many, of whom I have often told you and now tell you even with tears, live as enemies of the cross of Christ. Their end is destruction, their god is the belly, and they glory in their shame, with minds set on earthly things.
> —Philippians 3:18-20

In this hymn we ask God's help against the devil's temptations:

> *Help us keep the faith forever;*
> *Let not Satan, death, or shame*
> *Draw us from thee, or deprive us*
> *Of the honor of thy Name.*
> *When the foe would lure us hence*
> *Be thou, God, our sure defence.*
>
> —126 SBH

PRAYER

Dear heavenly Father: Keep me in your will and protect me from the temptations of my own mind and body. In Jesus' name. Amen. The Lord's Prayer.

"Give us this day our daily bread."

In all too many homes the family sits down at the table and begins to eat right away without a word of prayer, as though no one had anyone but himself to thank for the food. God is forgotten. But it is he who provides our "daily bread." No matter how hard we have worked or how much money we have, if God had not made the soil and caused the wheat to grow in it, we still would not have any bread to eat. Especially in these times, when there are hundreds of millions of people who do not have their daily bread, we ought to take time before each meal to remember that our food comes from God and to thank him for it. We should also ask God to forgive the greed and selfishness in the world that keep so many people from having the food that he provided and intended them to have.

Our Lord himself set the example for us of giving thanks to God for our daily bread:

> . . . the Lord Jesus on the night when he was betrayed took bread, and when he had given thanks, he broke it, and said, "This is my body which is for you. Do this in remembrance of me."
>
> —1 Corinthians 11:23-24

In this Thanksgiving hymn we recognize God as the one who makes things grow so that we can have our daily bread:

> *We plough the fields, and scatter*
> *The good seed on the land,*
> *But it is fed and watered*
> *By God's almighty hand;*
> *He sends the snow in winter,*
> *The warmth to swell the grain,*
> *The breezes and the sunshine,*
> *And soft refreshing rain.*
> *All good gifts around us*
> *Are sent from heaven above,*
> *Then thank the Lord, O thank the Lord,*
> *For all his love.*
>
> —364 SBH, 486 CSB

PRAYER

O God, our Creator and Provider: May I never sit down to eat without thanking you for my food. In Jesus' name. Amen. The Lord's Prayer.

"God gives daily bread, even without our prayer . . ."

God loves people enough to provide them with food even though they do not thank him for it or even stop to remember that it is he who gives it to them. Right now, in our country, God has given us such huge crops that we have food stored in warehouses all over the land. We have so much food that we actually don't know what to do with it. Of course, we do not have more food than the people of the world could eat—we simply have more than they can buy because millions of them are too poor to pay the prices that either we or their own countries charge them. Even though our government has sent food to other countries at low cost, or on credit, it often happens that their own corrupt officials or their lack of transportation prevents the people who need it most from getting it. All this is a great sin, and some day those responsible for it will be punished by God. But we will never be able to say that God did not provide enough food, even without our prayers.

The following favorite Thanksgiving prayer praises God as the giver of all that we need:

> The eyes of all look to thee,
>   and thou givest them their food
>   in due season.
> Thou openest thy hand,
>   thou satisfiest the desire of every
>   living thing.
> The Lord is just in all his ways,
>   and kind in all his doings.
>   —Psalm 145:15-17

This hymn continues the thought that God is the Provider of the things we need for life:

Come, ye thankful people, come,   *God our Maker doth provide*
Raise the song of harvest-home;   *For our wants to be supplied:*
All is safely gathered in   *Come, to God's own temple come,*
Ere the winter storms begin;   *Raise the song of harvest-home.*
                                       —363 SBH

PRAYER

O God, our Creator and Provider: I thank you that you are the Giver of every good and perfect gift. In Jesus' name. Amen. The Lord's Prayer.

Tuesday *The Fourth Petition*

". . . to all people, though sinful . . ."

We have said that millions of people do not have enough to eat. Many of them must be good, innocent people who are simply suffering from such things as wars and famines over which they have no control. On the other hand, there are many bad people who care nothing about God and who are making a fat living off others, and who have more than enough to eat. It does not seem fair that God would allow such things to go on. God does not want such things to happen—he has provided enough for everyone. If men are so selfish and grasping that everyone does not have enough, that is man's doing, not God's. God has created the world as man's living place and has provided enough of everything for everyone, even for those who do not believe in him or obey him. He loves all his children, just as earthly parents do, and he hopes that they will turn from their evil ways.

Jesus says that God provides even for wicked people, setting an example for us to love one another:

> But I say to you, Love your enemies and pray for those who persecute you, so that you may be sons of your Father who is in heaven; for he makes his sun rise on the evil and on the good, and sends rain on the just and on the unjust. For if you love those who love you, what reward have you?
> —Matthew 5:44-46a

All people on earth are asked in this hymn to praise God as the one who takes care of them:

> *All people that on earth do dwell,*
> *Sing to the Lord with cheerful voice;*
> *Him serve with mirth, his praise forth tell,*
> *Come ye before him, and rejoice.*
>
> *Know that the Lord is God indeed;*
> *Without our aid he did us make;*
> *We are his folk, he doth us feed,*
> *And for his sheep he doth us take.*
> —169 SBH

PRAYER

O God, our Creator and our Provider: I thank you for your great love and patience in wanting all men to be your children. Amen. The Lord's Prayer.

Wednesday   *The Fourth Petition*

". . . but we ask . . . that he will help us to realize this . . ."

When we say that we take something for granted, we mean that we are so sure of it that we do not bother to think very much about it or to be thankful for it. We often take the things our parents give us for granted, without ever thinking that they must work hard and sacrifice for us. So it is with the things God gives us. As we have said, many people never thank God for his blessings or think of him at all. But if we are Christians, we cannot act as though our blessings simply come out of the air. We know better. We know that all we have comes from our heavenly Father. Even though we may forget it once in a while, we must ask God not to let us forget it for very long. It is insulting to God and harmful to us to forget where our blessings come from.

The psalmist is reminding himself in these verses not to forget all that God has done for him:

> Bless the Lord, O my soul,
>   and forget not all his benefits,
> who forgives all your iniquity,
>   who heals all your diseases,
> who redeems your life from the Pit,
>   who crowns you with steadfast love and mercy,
> who satisfies you with good as long as you live.
> —Psalm 103:2-5a

Here is another hymn that invites us to praise and thank God for being our Provider:

> *Let us, with a gladsome mind,*
> *Praise the Lord, for he is kind.*
>
> *All things living he doth feed;*
> *His full hand supplies their need.*
>
> *He hath, with a piteous eye,*
> *Looked upon our misery:*
>
> Refrain:
>   *For his mercies aye endure,*
>   *Ever faithful, ever sure.*
> —405 SBH

PRAYER

O God, our Creator and our Provider: Help me to remember that everything I have is a gift from you. Amen. The Lord's Prayer.

Thursday   *The Fourth Petition*

". . . and to receive our daily bread with thanks."

It is not natural for human beings to be thankful. It is much more natural for us to forget our blessings, or take them for granted, than to count our blessings and be thankful for them. Then, too, we always want more than we have. We are always asking God for things in our prayers, and some of us pray only when there is something we want God to give us. It is a good habit for us to pray before meal time, because it teaches us that we do have something to be thankful for. If we have nothing else, we have our food, and that is really a great deal. We certainly could not live long without it. As Christians, we must begin to have a thankful feeling toward God rather than always to be asking and wanting. We must learn how to feel thankful for the commonest, most everyday things, like our daily bread.

The Bible reminds us to express our thanks to God, even when we are asking him for things:

> Have no anxiety about anything, but in everything by prayer and supplication with thanksgiving let your requests be made known to God. And the peace of God, which passes all understanding, will keep your hearts and your minds in Christ Jesus.
>
> —Philippians 4:6-7

In this Thanksgiving hymn we praise God for our daily bread and also ask him to give us spiritual food for our souls:

> *And now, on this our festal day,*
> *Thy bounteous hand confessing,*
> *Upon thine altar, Lord, we lay*
> *The first-fruits of thy blessing.*
> *By thee the souls of men are fed*
> *With gifts of grace supernal;*
> *Thou, who dost give us daily bread,*
> *Give us the bread eternal.*
>
> —445 SBH, 573 LH, 483 CSB

PRAYER

O God, our Creator and Provider: May I never forget that I always have my daily bread for which to be thankful. Amen. The Lord's Prayer.

191

Friday   *The Fourth Petition*

"Daily bread includes everything needed for this life . . ."

This is what Martin Luther believed Jesus meant when he told his disciples to pray for their daily bread—all the things needed for this life. The things needed for this life can be divided into two main classes: material and spiritual. Material things are those we can touch or see or smell or taste, like houses and clothes and coal and food. Our meditation today is about them. God knows that we could not live without such material things. That is why he has put the raw materials in the earth out of which we can make all the things we need. And that is why we should pray for them and be thankful for them. But we should always remember that God gives us these things so that we can live. We do not live in order to have these things. Some people think that is the purpose of life: to get things. But that is not God's purpose and it should not be ours. Our purpose is to serve him and one another.

The psalms paint beautiful word pictures of the material blessings of God:

> Thou crownest the year with thy bounty;
> the tracks of thy chariot drip with fatness.
> The pastures of the wilderness drip,
> the hills gird themselves with joy,
> the meadows clothe themselves with flocks,
> the valleys deck themselves with grain,
> they shout and sing together for joy.
> —Psalm 65:11-13

We recognize God as Creator and Provider of our material needs in this harvest hymn:

> *Lord, in thy Name thy servants plead,*
> *And thou hast sworn to hear;*
> *Thine is the harvest, thine the seed,*
> *The fresh and fading year.*
>
> *Our hope, when autumn winds blew wild,*
> *We trusted, Lord, with thee;*
> *And now, when spring has on us smiled,*
> *We wait on thy decree.*
>
> —362 SBH

PRAYER

O God, our Creator and Provider: I thank you for all the material things of life. May they help me to serve you better. Amen. The Lord's Prayer.

"Daily bread includes everything needed for this life . . ."

Yesterday we talked about material things that were necessary for this life. But we said there were spiritual things that we need too. Spiritual things cannot be touched or seen or tasted; but they are very real nevertheless. Love and faith and happiness and friendship—these are spiritual things, but you will agree that they are real and that they are most necessary for life. Luther says that these are also included when we pray for our daily bread. If we have a good home, a strong faith, a loving family, friends who share our happiness and our sadness; if we have good health; if we live in a free country; if we have fine neighbors—all these make a difference in our lives, and we should remember that these things also come from God, who knows that we need them and wants us to have them.

The Bible reminds us that all the blessings of this life are from God:

> Every good endowment and every perfect gift is from above, coming down from the Father of lights with whom there is no variation or shadow due to change.
> —James 1:17

This famous hymn asks God to satisfy our spiritual needs of life as well as our material needs:

> *Break thou the bread of life,*
> *Dear Lord, to me,*
> *As thou didst break the loaves*
> *Beside the sea;*
> *Beyond the sacred page*
> *I seek thee, Lord;*
> *My spirit pants for thee,*
> *O living Word!*
> —491 SBH

PRAYER

O God, our Creator and Provider: I thank you for the spiritual things of life. May I always consider them your most precious gifts to me. Amen. The Lord's Prayer.

Sunday *The Fifth Petition*

". . . and forgive us our trespasses . . ."

To trespass means to intrude or to go beyond what is lawful. It is like walking on someone's well-kept lawn instead of on the sidewalk where we are supposed to walk. We are supposed to walk in God's way, but we are always trespassing, always stepping off God's straight and narrow way, and going where we are not supposed to. Because we do this, we need God's forgiveness. We should really feel the need for his forgiveness. We should feel it deep down in our hearts and minds. It is the most important feeling a Christian can have, because it sets his whole thinking straight. If we sincerely feel the need for God's forgiveness, then we can never become proud; we can never think we are better than others. And we will always know that we need our Lord Jesus, who died in order that our sins could be forgiven.

The Apostle John tells us of our need to be forgiven:

> If we say we have no sin, we deceive ourselves, and the truth is not in us. If we confess our sins, he is faithful and just, and will forgive our sins and cleanse us from all unrighteousness.
>
> —1 John 1:8-9

We ask God's forgiveness in this hymn:

> *God of pity, God of grace:*
> *When we humbly seek Thy face,*
> *Bend from heaven, Thy dwelling-place:*
> *Hear, forgive, and save.*
>
> *Should we wander from Thy fold,*
> *And our love to Thee grow cold,*
> *With a pitying eye behold:*
> *Lord, forgive and save.*
>
> —278, CSB

PRAYER

Dear heavenly Father: Help me at all times to feel the need for the forgiveness of my sins. For Jesus' sake, Amen. The Lord's Prayer.

Monday   *The Fifth Petition*

"... as we forgive those who trespass against us."

If we are not careful, we may come to think that our Christianity is simply a matter between God and us. For instance, we think that as long as God forgives our sins, that is all that counts. But Christianity goes farther than God and us. It is also a matter between us and other people. We cannot love God and hate our fellow human beings. We cannot be humble toward God and proud toward other people. If we think we can lead that kind of double life, God tells us right away we are wrong. Jesus tells us that before we lay our gifts on God's altar, we must first make things right with our brother. If we pray God to forgive us our sins against him, we must be willing to forgive the wrong others do to us. It might take a long time to get ourselves to that place, but it is the only way we can show God that we really mean our Christianity.

Jesus tells us that forgiveness is a two-way thing:

> For if you forgive men their trespasses, your heavenly Father also will forgive you; but if you do not forgive men their trespasses, neither will your Father forgive your trespasses.
>
> —Matthew 6:14-15

In this hymn we ask God to give us forgiving hearts, like his:

> *O for a heart to praise my God,*
> *A heart from sin set free!*
> *A heart that always feels thy Blood*
> *So freely shed for me;*
>
> *A heart in every thought renewed*
> *And full of love divine;*
> *Perfect, and right, and pure, and good,*
> *A copy, Lord, of thine.*
>
> —389 SBH, 264 CSB

PRAYER

Dear heavenly Father: Give me patience, love, and humility enough to forgive others as you have forgiven me. For Jesus' sake. Amen. The Lord's Prayer.

Tuesday   *The Fifth Petition*

"We ask in this prayer that our Father in heaven would not hold our sins against us and because of them refuse to hear our prayer."

When we ask someone to forgive us, we want that person to hold against us no longer the wrong that we did him. We want him to believe that we will do differently from now on, that we will turn over a new leaf. We want things to be as they were before we did the wrong. That is what we ask God in this petition of the Lord's Prayer. The difference is that we cannot ask God to forgive and no longer hold our sins against us for our sakes. We can only ask him to do it for Jesus' sake, who died for our sins. If we believe in him as our Savior, God will forgive our sins and allow us to start each day with a clean slate. If God would not forgive our sins, we could not come before him with our prayers, because we would have no right to do so. But because of Christ's sacrifice for us, God is always willing to hear us and wants us to come to him in prayer.

Life's greatest blessing is to feel forgiven by God:

> In thee, O Lord, do I seek refuge;
> let me never be put to shame;
> in thy righteousness deliver me!
> Incline thy ear to me,
> rescue me speedily!
> Be thou a rock of refuge for me,
> a strong fortress to save me!
>
> —Psalm 31:1-2

We ask God, in this hymn, to forgive us for Jesus' sake:

> *With broken heart and contrite sigh,*
> *A trembling sinner, Lord, I cry;*
> *Thy pardoning grace is rich and free:*
> *O God, be merciful to me.*
>
> *Nor alms, nor deeds that I have done,*
> *Can for a single sin atone;*
> *To Calvary alone I flee:*
> *O God, be merciful to me.*
>
> —367 SBH, 323 LH, 316 CSB

PRAYER

Dear heavenly Father: I thank you that because my sins are forgiven I can come to you and you will hear me, for Jesus' sake. Amen. The Lord's Prayer.

Wednesday   *The Fifth Petition*

"And we pray that he would give us everything by grace . . ."

The word "grace" is a favorite Christian word. It is used in our worship services, in our prayers, and in the New Testament. Hardly a sermon is ever preached in a Lutheran church without the minister's using it. Still, like so many other words we use often, we probably don't know its real meaning. We could say that God's grace is his love. But that would not tell the whole story. We could say that grace is doing something for someone as a pure favor. That is not the full meaning either. God's grace to us is more than loving us or doing us a favor—it is loving and doing a favor for disobedient, sinful people. It is one thing to love your friend, but quite another thing to love your enemy. God's grace means he loves us even though we sin against him and disobey him. Even when the people of Jesus' time nailed him to a cross, he said, "Father, forgive them." That is what grace means and that is why we should always feel thankful to God for it.

In this Bible verse we have one of the most important teachings of our Protestant faith:

> For by grace you have been saved through faith; and this is not your own doing, it is the gift of God.
> —Ephesians 2:8

We praise God for his grace in this hymn:

> *Give to our God immortal praise,*
> *Mercy and truth are all his ways.*
> *Wonders of grace to God belong,*
> *Repeat his mercies in your song.*
>
> *He sent his Son with power to save*
> *From guilt and darkness and the grave.*
> *Wonders of grace to God belong,*
> *Repeat his mercies in your song.*
> —441 SBH, 307 CSB

PRAYER

Dear heavenly Father: I thank you for the gift of your grace to me, a sinner. For Jesus' sake. Amen. The Lord's Prayer.

Thursday *The Fifth Petition*

"For we sin every day and deserve nothing but punishment."

None of us, when we pray, can ask God to give us what we deserve or what we have coming. If we deliver newspapers, we can ask our customers for the money we have coming; or if our parents promise us an allowance for doing chores around the house, we can say that we deserve the money if we actually do the work. But we really do not deserve or have coming all the blessings of God, for we could not possibly earn them because we disobey his will by thought, word, and deed. It is only through God's grace or his fatherly love that he gives us everything we have.

We should always come to God confessing our sins, rather than demanding anything. The psalms have some beautiful prayers of confession:

> For I know my transgressions,
>   and my sin is ever before me.
> Against thee, thee only, have I sinned,
>   and done that which is evil in thy sight.
>   —Psalm 51:3-4

In this hymn, often sung before receiving the Lord's Supper, we tell God we have no right to come to him at all, but that we come only because of his love and forgiveness:

> *Just as I am, without one plea,*
> *But that thy Blood was shed for me,*
> *And that thou bidd'st me come to thee,*
>   *O Lamb of God, I come, I come.*

> *Just as I am, thou wilt receive,*
> *Wilt welcome, pardon, cleanse, relieve;*
> *Because thy promise I believe,*
>   *O Lamb of God, I come, I come.*
>   —370 SBH, 388 LH, 337 CSB

PRAYER

Dear heavenly Father: I am thankful that you do not give me what I deserve, but that you give me blessings instead. For Jesus' sake. Amen. The Lord's Prayer.

Friday   *The Fifth Petition*

"So we on our part will heartily forgive and gladly do good to those who sin against us."

Here we come to one of the hardest parts of Christianity: forgiving those who do us wrong. That is one reason why there are not more Christians in the world. People simply cannot bring themselves to forgive their enemies. That is also why history is full of wars. All of us want others to forgive us, but we do not want to forgive others. Luther reminds us that as Christians we must not only forgive, but heartily forgive. Heartily means from the heart. In other words, we are to put our hearts into forgiving others, and not just say that we forgive them, but really mean it. We must no longer hold any grudges or think evil thoughts about them. We will need God's help to do this, and we will have to pray about it often.

Jesus told Peter that there should be no limit to forgiving others:

> Then Peter came up and said to him, "Lord, how often shall my brother sin against me, and I forgive him? As many as seven times?" Jesus said to him, "I do not say to you seven times, but seventy times seven."
>
> —Matthew 18:21-22

In this Holy Week hymn we ask for a forgiving heart as Jesus had toward those who did wrong to him:

> *Saviour, for our pardon sue,*
> *When our sins thy pangs renew,*
> *For we know not what we do:*
>   *Hear us, holy Jesus.*
>
> *O may we, who mercy need,*
> *Be like thee in heart and deed,*
> *When with wrong our spirits bleed:*
>   *Hear us, holy Jesus.*
>
> 81 SBH, 180 LH, 84 CSB

PRAYER

Dear heavenly Father: Make me a strong enough Christian to forgive with my heart as well as with my lips. For Jesus' sake. Amen. The Lord's Prayer.

"... and gladly do good to those who sin against us."

Forgiving those who wrong us may be very difficult; but we are asked to go even a step farther than that: we are asked actually to do good to them! Once we become Christians, that is, followers of Christ, we have to look at things in new and different ways. When people are not followers of Christ, their only thought is to get revenge on those who hurt them. They think only of themselves. Christ wants us to think of the other person. By doing good to those who harm us or hurt our pride or gossip about us, we might change their attitude; and because of our example, they might also become followers of Christ. An American soldier who died in a Japanese prison camp requested before he died that the war bonds he had saved be used to send a Japanese soldier to an American school to learn our way of life. We are not only to forgive and then forget; we are also to help.

Jesus taught us a completely new way of dealing with people who sin against us:

> But I say to you that hear, Love your enemies, do good to those who hate you, bless those who curse you, pray for those who abuse you.
>
> —Luke 6:27-28

We ask God's strength in this hymn to do the things he wants and that Jesus taught us to do:

> *Order my footsteps by Thy Word,*
> *And make my heart sincere;*
> *Let sin have no dominion, Lord,*
> *But keep my conscience clear.*
>
> *Assist my soul, too apt to stray,*
> *A stricter watch to keep;*
> *And should I e'er forget Thy way,*
> *Restore Thy wandering sheep.*
>
> —275, CSB

PRAYER

Dear heavenly Father: Give me a love that will do good to those who have done wrong to me, even as you have done good to me. For Jesus' sake. Amen. The Lord's Prayer.

". . . and lead us not into temptation."

Temptation really means a test to see whether we are going to choose to do what is bad or what is good. In almost everything we do we have the chance to follow the evil way or the good way—God's way. We are always being tested, or tempted. We always have a choice. What we are praying in this petition is not that God would get us out of these tests, these temptations, as our teacher sometimes excuses us from taking a test in some subject. God would have to change the world to do that, because as long as we are in the world, and as long as evil is in the world, we will be tempted to do what is evil. What we pray in this petition is that God will not let us fail our tests; that he will not let us take the evil way, but keep us on the good path.

The Bible encourages us to ask Jesus for help when we are tempted, because he himself was tested in this way:

> For we have not a high priest who is unable to sympathize with our weaknesses, but one who in every respect has been tempted as we are, yet without sinning. Let us then with confidence draw near to the throne of grace, that we may receive mercy and find grace to help in time of need.
> —Hebrews 4:15-16

The following hymn also expresses the theme of being helped in our temptations by the example of Jesus, who was also tempted:

Christian, dost thou see them
On the holy ground,
How the powers of darkness
Compass thee around?
Christian, up and smite them,
Counting gain but loss;
Smite them by the merit
Of the holy Cross.

Well I know thy trouble,
O my servant true,
Thou art very weary,
I was weary too;
But that toil shall make thee
Some day all mine own,
And the end of sorrow
Shall be near my throne.

—68 SBH

PRAYER

Dear Lord Jesus: I know that you can help me when I am tempted to sin, because you were also tempted. Make me strong as you are strong. Amen. The Lord's Prayer.

Monday   *The Sixth Petition*

"God tempts no one to sin . . ."

It would be hard to imagine a parent who would on purpose tempt his children to do what is wrong. Some Christian people believe that God actually brings them temptations just to see if they are strong enough to fight them off. Our heavenly Father does not want us to be tempted any more than our earthly parents do. God would be most happy if his children were not tempted at all. But everyone in the world, including Christians, is tempted because of evil in the world. Therefore God cannot take away temptation, but he can and does give his children faith and courage and strength to overcome temptation. Not only that— by helping us to overcome evil he makes us stronger and wiser and more faithful than we were before. If we put our trust in him, God will turn even what is evil into good for us.

St. James reminds us that God does not tempt us, but our own desire tempts us to give in to what is evil:

> Let no one say when he is tempted, "I am tempted by God"; for God cannot be tempted with evil and he himself tempts no one; but each person is tempted when he is lured and enticed by his own desire.
>
> —James 1:13-14

In this hymn we ask Jesus' help in time of temptation:

> *If the way be drear,*
> *If the foe be near,*
> *Let not faithless fears o'ertake us,*
> *Let not faith and hope forsake us;*
> *For through many a foe*
> *To our home we go.*
>
> *When we seek relief*
> *From a long-felt grief,*
> *When temptations come alluring*
> *Make us patient and enduring;*
> *Show us that bright shore*
> *Where we weep no more.*
>
> —532 SBH, 260 CSB

PRAYER

Dear Lord Jesus: Give me strength and courage to overcome temptation and to grow in my faith. Amen. The Lord's Prayer.

Tuesday   *The Sixth Petition*

"... that God would watch over us so that the devil, the world, and our sinful self may not deceive us ..."

The closer we come to God and the more we live according to his commandments, the easier it is for us to tell right from wrong. People who do not know God and his commandments hardly know the difference between right and wrong, good and evil. But no matter how close to God we are, the devil never gives up trying to deceive us. To deceive a person means to fool him. The devil is the world's greatest deceiver. He fools us into thinking that what is bad for us is really good for us; he fools us into believing we want to think and say and do things that we really do not want to think and say and do at all. He fools us into believing that we are happier when we follow him than when we follow God. That is why we must always be on guard and pray to God for wisdom so that we will not be deceived by the devil.

St. Paul told the Christians in Ephesus that faith in God is the best protection against the devil's temptations:

> ... above all taking the shield of faith, with which you can quench all the flaming darts of the evil one.
> —Ephesians 6:16

In this hymn we look to Jesus as our Protector against the devil:

> *Though Satan's wrath beset our path*
> *And worldly scorn assail us,*
> *While Thou art near we will not fear:*
> *Thy strength shall never fail us.*
> *Thy rod and staff shall keep us safe,*
> *And guide our steps for ever;*
> *Nor shades of death, nor hell beneath,*
> *Our souls from Thee shall sever.*
> —334, CSB, 437 LH

PRAYER

Dear Lord Jesus: I pray for wisdom so that the devil may not be able to deceive me. Amen. The Lord's Prayer.

". . . so that the devil, the world, and our sinful self may not . . . draw us into unbelief . . ."

The worst thing that could ever happen to us would be for us to become unbelievers and lose our faith in God and in his love for us. This is always the devil's aim, and he works through the world and our sinful selves to get us to give up our faith. Some lose their faith by becoming angry or disappointed with their church or someone in the church. Others have work to do on Sundays, and gradually they leave their church and their faith. Still others become friends with people who have no faith, and soon they lose theirs too. And sometimes serious illness or the death of a loved one causes people to become unbelievers. In such circumstances we must recognize the devil at work, and we must ask God for strength to keep our faith.

The father of a boy whom Jesus healed had to ask Jesus for help to believe, as we sometimes have to do:

> And Jesus said to him, ". . . All things are possible to him who believes." Immediately the father of the child cried out and said, "I believe; help my unbelief!"
>
> —Mark 9:23-24

In this hymn we ask God for a strong faith:

> *O for a faith that will not shrink,*
> *Though pressed by many a foe,*
> *That will not tremble on the brink*
> *Of poverty or woe;*
>
> *That will not murmur nor complain*
> *Beneath the chastening rod,*
> *But in the hour of grief or pain*
> *Can lean upon its God.*
>
> —395 SBH, 266 CSB

PRAYER

Dear Lord Jesus: Help me to keep my belief in you, and may it grow stronger day by day. Amen. The Lord's Prayer.

Thursday   *The Sixth Petition*

". . . so that the devil, the world, and our sinful self may not . . . draw us into . . . despair . . ."

If the devil cannot fool us in any other way, he tries to make us believe that there is no use trying to fight temptation, that God has let us down, and that we might as well give up, or despair. When God does not answer our prayers right away or when we have been sick for a long time, or when we are having a lot of trouble with our school work, then we must remember that even the greatest Christians have had their discouraging trials; but God has always finally come to their rescue and turned their despair into happiness and hope. This should give us courage to hang on to our faith in God, no matter how hard the devil tries to make us let go.

When we are tempted to despair, here is one of the most helpful passages we can read:

> No temptation has overtaken you that is not common to man. God is faithful, and he will not let you be tempted beyond your strength, but with the temptation will also provide the way of escape, that you may be able to endure it.
> —1 Corinthians 10:13

We tell ourselves in this hymn that because we are God's people he will lead us through despair and doubt:

> *Through the night of doubt and sorrow*
> *Onward goes the pilgrim band,*
> *Singing songs of expectation,*
> *Marching to the promised land.*

> *One the light of God's own presence*
> *O'er his ransomed people shed,*
> *Chasing far the gloom and terror,*
> *Brightening all the path we tread:*
> —529 SBH, 481 LH, 201 CSB

PRAYER

Dear Lord Jesus: Help me to believe that you will never allow me to be tempted beyond my strength if I am faithful to you. Amen. The Lord's Prayer.

Friday   *The Sixth Petition*

". . . may not draw us into . . . other great and shameful sins."

Any daily newspaper carries a number of examples of "great and shameful sins" done by human beings. In fact, much of the time the great and shameful sins, like killing or robbing or lying, are the events that make the headlines. What makes people do such things? Often those who do them are from good homes and families or have important and respected positions in society. The answer is that if the devil tried to tempt Jesus himself to sin, we must all expect to be tempted, no matter who we are. And unless we have God's help, any one of us can fall into great and shameful sin. We must never think we are so good that God does not have to watch over us.

The Bible warns us that great and shameful sins will keep us out of God's kingdom:

> Be sure of this, that no immoral or impure man, or one who is covetous (that is, an idolator), has any inheritance in the kingdom of Christ and of God. Let no one deceive you with empty words, for it is because of these things that the wrath of God comes upon the sons of disobedience.
> —Ephesians 5:5-6

In this hymn we ask God to keep us from sin:

> *Breathe on me, Breath of God,*
> *Fill me with life anew,*
> *That I may love what thou dost love,*
> *And do what thou wouldst do.*
>
> *Breathe on me, Breath of God,*
> *Until my heart is pure,*
> *Until with thee I will one will,*
> *To do and to endure.*
>
> —470 SBH

PRAYER

Dear Lord Jesus: Help me to love you so much that I will not want to do anything that is against your will. Amen. The Lord's Prayer.

Saturday *The Sixth Petition*

"... we pray that ... we may still win the final victory."

Success in anything takes a lot of hard trying. If we want to win a race or be a star basketball or football player, we must keep our body in the best possible shape and spend many hours in faithful practice. If we want to be a success in our life's work, it means either many years of study, or actual experience on the job, or both. Success never comes easy. That is why, if we are going to be successful in our fight against temptation—if we are going to win—we can never let up. God gives us the strength to win over temptation, but only if we keep on trying with all our might. Luther talks about "the final victory," because he knew from personal experience that most of the time victory over temptation does not come right away. It may take us a long time to learn to control our temper, or to tell the truth even when it may hurt us. But finally, if we keep trying, God will help us to win. And that is what counts.

St. Paul compares the Christian life to a race:

> Do you not know that in a race all the runners compete, but only one receives the prize? So run that you may obtain it. Every athlete exercises self-control in all things. They do it to receive a perishable wreath, but we an imperishable.
> —1 Corinthians 9:24-25

In this Easter hymn we sing that because Christ has won the victory over sin and death, his victory will be ours if we believe in him:

> *The Day of Resurrection,*
> *Earth, tell it out abroad;*
> *The Passover of gladness,*
> *The Passover of God!*
> *From death to life eternal,*
> *From earth unto the sky,*
> *Our Christ hath brought us over*
> *With hymns of victory.*
> —105 SBH, 115 CSB

PRAYER

Dear Lord Jesus: Keep me faithful so that I will be able to share in your victory over sin and death. Amen. The Lord's Prayer.

"But deliver us from evil."

In this case the word "deliver" means to save. We pray that God will save us from all evil. That does not mean that nothing evil will ever happen to us. Christians must go through their share of hardships and suffering like everyone, because all of us live in the world and the world is full of evil. To go through this life without having any evil happen to you would be like going swimming without getting wet. It cannot be done. But we pray that no matter what does happen, it will not take us away from God or make us lose our faith. We pray for strength to overcome hardship and evil, and that such things may bring us closer to him than ever.

Jesus tells us that he is strong enough to deliver us from all the world's evil:

> In the world you have tribulation; but be of good cheer,
> I have overcome the world.
> —John 16:33b

In this hymn we ask Jesus to deliver us from losing our faith or committing sin:

> *In the hour of trial,*
> *Jesus, plead for me,*
> *Lest by base denial*
> *I depart from thee;*
> *When thou seest me waver,*
> *With a look recall,*
> *Nor from fear or favor,*
> *Suffer me to fall.*
>
> *With forbidden pleasures*
> *Should this vain world charm,*
> *Or its sordid treasures*
> *Spread to work me harm,*
> *Bring to my remembrance*
> *Sad Gethsemane,*
> *Or, in darker semblance,*
> *Cross-crowned Calvary.*
> —561 SBH, 516 LH

PRAYER

Dear Lord Jesus: I do not ask to be excused from temptation and difficulty, but I ask for strength to stay faithful to you. Amen. The Lord's Prayer.

Monday   *The Seventh Petition*

"... and at our last hour ..."

There are some people who brag about the fact that they do not believe anything. But there is one thing which all of us will have to believe, whether we admit it or not, and that is death. All of us will have to die sometime. When God created Adam and Eve, he made them so that they would live forever; but when they disobeyed God, they brought sin into the world. With sin came death. Many years ago people looked for the "fountain of youth," which was said to have water that would make a person live forever. We know that there is no such fountain. We know that none of us can run away from death. That ought to make us want to live in such a way that we will be ready at any time to leave this world and meet our heavenly Father.

The end of the world comes for each one when he dies. Jesus warns us to be ready:

> Watch therefore—for you do not know when the master of the house will come, in the evening, or at midnight, or at cockcrow, or in the morning—lest he come suddenly and find you asleep. And what I say to you I say to all: Watch.
> —Mark 13:35-37

In this hymn we say that we are ready for death because we trust in Jesus:

> *Green pastures are before me,*
> *Which yet I have not seen;*
> *Bright skies will soon be o'er me,*
> *Where darkest clouds have been.*
> *My hope I cannot measure,*
> *The path to life is free;*
> *My Saviour has my treasure,*
> *And he will walk with me.*
>
> —574 SBH

PRAYER

Dear Lord Jesus: Help me to learn to trust you in all things, so that when my last hour comes I will trust you even then. Amen. The Lord's Prayer.

". . . mercifully take us from the troubles of this world . . ."

This world and this life are not what God wants them to be. He does not want people killing each other in wars. He does not want boys and girls to go hungry as they do in India and China. He does not want homes to break up because of divorce or people to be kept from a decent life because their skin is colored. All these are troubles that sinful people bring into the world because they go against God's will. But the Bible promises us that those who believe in Jesus and who try to do his will here on earth will have a happy life with him forever, without any troubles.

In St. John's vision of heaven he hears God say that he will take all our troubles away:

> . . . and I heard a great voice from the throne saying, "Behold, the dwelling of God is with men. He will dwell with them, and they shall be his people, and God himself will be with them; he will wipe away every tear from their eyes, and death shall be no more, neither shall there be mourning nor crying nor pain any more, for the former things have passed away."
>
> —Revelation 21:3-4

Some of our hymns picture the joys of a life after death without troubles:

> *There is a land of pure delight,*
> *Where saints immortal reign;*
> *Infinite day excludes the night,*
> *And pleasures banish pain.*
>
> *There everlasting spring abides,*
> *And never-withering flowers;*
> *Death, like a narrow sea, divides*
> *This heavenly land from ours.*
>
> —583 SBH, 518 CSB

PRAYER

Dear Lord Jesus: Help me to bear up under the troubles of this world, because I know that some day I will be with you. Amen. The Lord's Prayer.

210

Wednesday   *The Seventh Petition*

"... mercifully take us ... to himself in heaven."

If someone were to ask you, "What is Christianity all about?" could you give a good, short answer? As truthful an answer as any would be this: "Christianity is about God's trying to get us back to himself." We all know by this time that the first people God created wanted to go their own way. Instead of loving God, they loved what was evil. And from that time until now God has been working to win mankind back to himself, because he loves us and wants us for his own children. That is why God came down to earth in the form of a human being, so that he could show us the way to heaven and to himself. And that is why he suffered on the cross for our sins, so that not even sin could keep us from him.

Jesus tells us that he himself will prepare for us a place in heaven:

> In my Father's house are many rooms; if it were not so, would I have told you that I go to prepare a place for you? And when I go and prepare a place for you, I will come again and will take you to myself, that where I am you may be also.
>
> —John 14:2-3

A child asks Jesus in this lovely hymn to take him to heaven:

> *Through this day thy hand has led me,*
>   *And I thank thee for thy care;*
> *Thou hast warmed me, clothed and fed me,*
>   *Listen to my evening prayer.*
>
> *Let my sins be all forgiven;*
>   *Bless the friends I love so well;*
> *Take me, Lord, at last to heaven,*
>   *Happy there with thee to dwell.*
>
> —235 SBH, 577 CSB

PRAYER

Dear Lord Jesus: I pray that when my life on earth is done, I may live with you in your wonderful home. Amen. The Lord's Prayer.

Thursday *The Doxology*

"For thine is the kingdom and the power and the glory forever and ever."

The important word in this conclusion to the Lord's Prayer is "the": the Kingdom, the power, and the glory. When we say the President, everyone knows we mean the President of the United States, or the most important President there is, at least to us. When we say, "I'm going to see the boss," we don't mean the boss of some department or floor; we mean the boss of the whole company. And so, when we say, "For thine is the kingdom and the power and the glory," we mean that God's kingdom and power and glory are the only ones that count: his is greater than all the rest. And more than that, his are "forever and ever," long after the other kingdoms and powers and glories are dead and gone. What a wonderful God!

The Second Psalm reminds the powerful people of the world that God's kingdom and power and glory are greater than theirs:

> Now therefore, O kings, be wise;
> be warned, O rulers of the earth.
> Serve the Lord with fear,
> with trembling kiss his feet,
> lest he be angry, and you perish in the way;
> for his wrath is quickly kindled.
> —Psalm 2:10-12

One of our beloved Christian hymns tells Jesus that our highest praise is for him:

> *Beautiful Saviour,*
> *Lord of the nations,*
> *Son of God and Son of Man!*
> *Glory and honor,*
> *Praise, adoration,*
> *Now and for evermore be thine!*
> 434 SBH, 657 LH, 129 CSB

PRAYER

Dear Lord Jesus: I pray that you may always be the king of my heart. Amen. The Lord's Prayer.

Friday   *The Doxology*

"*Amen* means *yes, it shall be so.*"

The Lord's Prayer has that name because Jesus taught it to his disciples when they asked him how they should pray. It has often been called "the perfect prayer," and every Christian certainly ought to know it by heart. But it is not enough to know the Lord's Prayer by heart, or to know the Creed by heart, or to know any other part of our Christian faith; we must also believe it. There is no good whatsoever that can come from simply reciting the Lord's Prayer as if it were so many magic words. We must believe in our hearts that what we pray is true, and that God really hears us. That is why, at the end, we say "Amen." It means that we believe what we have just said.

The New Testament ends with two "Amens," to show that the men who wrote it believed in Jesus with all their hearts:

> He who testifies to these things says, "Surely I am coming soon." Amen. Come, Lord Jesus! The grace of the Lord Jesus be with all the saints. Amen.
>
> —Revelation 22:20-21

The *Service Book and Hymnal* of our church has an "Amen" after hymns of prayer and praise to show that we sincerely mean what we sing:

> *Prayer is the Christian's vital breath,*
> *The Christian's native air,*
> *His watchword at the gates of death:*
> *He enters heaven with prayer.*
>
> *O thou by whom we come to God,*
> *The Life, the Truth, the Way,*
> *The path of prayer thyself hast trod:*
> *Lord, teach us how to pray. Amen.*
>
> —458 SBH

PRAYER

Dear Lord Jesus: May my prayers never be just words, but the honest wishes and beliefs of my heart. Amen. The Lord's Prayer.

Saturday *The Doxology*

"For he himself ... has promised to hear us."

When a pastor talks with people about prayer, one of the questions they often ask is, "How can I be sure that God really hears my prayers?" Most people who have not had much experience with Christianity want proof first, and then they will have faith. But God does not work that way. He wants us to have faith, to believe in his promises, first—then he will give us all the proof we need. He has promised us through his Holy Word that he will hear our prayers and that he will answer them, provided, of course, they are not foolish prayers. So we must take God at his word; we must believe in him; we must have faith in him. Then, when we look back over our life, we will see how God did answer our prayers. That is the proof that every real Christian has.

Jesus definitely promises us that God will hear our prayers and do something about them:

> Whatever you ask in my name, I will do it, that the Father may be glorified in the Son; if you ask anything in my name, I will do it.
>
> —John 14:13-14

In this hymn we accept Jesus' invitation to come to him in prayer:

> *Come, my soul, thy suit prepare:*
> *Jesus loves to answer prayer;*
> *He Himself has bid thee pray,*
> *Therefore will not say thee nay.*

> *Thou art coming to a King:*
> *Large petitions with thee bring;*
> *For His grace and power are such,*
> *None can ever ask too much.*
> —277, CSB, 459 LH

PRAYER

Dear Lord Jesus: I believe that you hear me when I pray and that you will answer my prayers in the way that is best for me. Amen. The Lord's Prayer.

214

PART FOUR

The Sacrament of Baptism

1

*What is
Baptism?*

The sacrament of Baptism it not water
    only,
but it is water used together with God's
    Word and by his command.

*What is
this Word?*

*In Matthew 28 our Lord Jesus Christ
    says:*
"Go therefore and make disciples of all
    nations,
baptizing them in the name of the
    Father and of the Son and of the Holy
    Spirit."

2

*What benefits
does God give
in Baptism?*

In Baptism God forgives sin,
delivers from death and the devil,
and gives everlasting salvation to all who
    believe what he has promised.

*What is
God's promise?*

In Mark 16 our Lord Jesus Christ says:
"He who believes and is baptized will be
    saved;
but he who does not believe will be
    condemned."

3

*How can water
do such
great things?*

It is not water that does these things,
but God's Word with the water and our
    trust in this Word.
Water by itself is only water,
but with this Word it is a life-giving
    water
which by grace gives the new birth
    through the Holy Spirit.

St. Paul writes in Titus 3:
"He saved us . . . in virtue of his own
    mercy,
by the washing of regeneration and
    renewal in the Holy Spirit,
which he poured out upon us richly
through Jesus Christ our Savior,
so that we might be justified by his grace
and become heirs in hope of eternal life.
The saying is sure."

4

*What does
Baptism mean
for daily
living?*

It means that our sinful self, with all its
    evil deeds and desires,
should be drowned through daily
    repentance;
and that day after day a new self should
    arise
to live with God in righteousness and
    purity forever.

St. Paul writes in Romans 6:
"We were buried therefore with him by
    Baptism into death,
so that as Christ was raised from the
    dead by the glory of the Father,
we too might walk in newness of life."

The Sacrament of Baptism

"He saved us . . . in virtue of his own mercy . . ."

Let us suppose you have been saved from drowning by a friend. You would never be able to look at life in quite the same way again. First, your life would seem more precious to you than ever before. We usually don't realize the value of things until we think we are going to lose them. Second, you would feel you could never repay your friend for what he did for you. That is exactly how every Christian ought to feel. We have been saved from death as surely as if we had been drowning—a more awful death than drowning: an everlasting death apart from God. So we ought to be forever thankful to Jesus because "he saved us in virtue of his mercy."

The first name given to Jesus after he was born was "Savior":

> And the angel said to them, "Be not afraid; for behold, I bring you good news of a great joy which will come to all the people; for to you is born this day in the city of David a Savior, who is Christ the Lord."
>
> —Luke 2:10-11

We call Jesus "Savior" in many of our hymns, like this favorite of children:

> *Saviour, like a shepherd lead us,*
> *Much we need thy tender care;*
> *In thy pleasant pastures feed us,*
> *For our use thy folds prepare:*
> *Blessed Jesus*
> *Thou hast bought us: thine we are.*
>
> —524 SBH, 565 CSB

PRAYER

Dear Lord and Savior: I am grateful that you have saved me so I can be with you forever. Amen. The Lord's Prayer.

Monday   *The Sacrament of Baptism*

"... by the washing of regeneration ..."

The "washing of regeneration" is another name for Baptism. We all know that when we wash something we make it clean. But in the case of Baptism we are not made clean on the outside, but on the inside—we are made spiritually clean. We put it in another way when we say that we are "born again," spiritually speaking. Our spirits need to be washed by Baptism because even when we are little babies, our spirits do not follow God's Spirit. Just as soon as we are old enough to walk and talk and want things, we do not go God's way—we go our own way. In Baptism God washes our spirit so that if our parents bring us up in the right way, our spirit will want to do God's will. Without Baptism our spirits can never do God's will.

Jesus tells us that Baptism is necessary for our salvation:

> Jesus answered, "Truly, truly, I say to you, unless one is born anew, he cannot see the kingdom of God ... unless one is born of water and the Spirit, he cannot enter the kingdom of God."
>
> —John 3:3, 5

We sing about Baptism and salvation in this hymn:

> *He that believes and is baptized*
> *Shall see the Lord's salvation;*
> *Baptized into the death of Christ,*
> *He is a new creation;*
> *Through Christ's redemption he shall stand*
> *Among the glorious heavenly band*
> *Of every tribe and nation.*
>
> *With one accord, O God, we pray;*
> *Grant us thy Holy Spirit;*
> *Look thou on our infirmity*
> *Through Jesus' Blood and merit;*
> *Grant us to grow in grace each day*
> *By holy baptism, that we may*
> *Eternal life inherit. Amen.*
>
> —259 SBH

PRAYER

Dear Lord Jesus: I am grateful for being baptized and for living in a Christian home. Amen. The Lord's Prayer.

Tuesday   *The Sacrament of Baptism*

". . . and renewal in the Holy Spirit . . ."

In Baptism our spirit is washed clean by God. Something else happens too: God's own Spirit, the Holy Spirit, comes into our hearts and begins to guide us into the way he wants us to go. In the explanation to the third article of the Creed we learned: "I believe that I cannot by my own understanding or effort believe in Jesus Christ, my Lord or come to him. But the Holy Spirit has called me through the gospel, enlightened me with his gifts, and sanctified and kept me in true faith." It is in Baptism that the Holy Spirit enters our hearts and begins to sanctify us, or make us holy; and as time goes on he helps us to grow and be stronger in the true faith of God. In other words, the Holy Spirit renews us, makes us new people, true children of God.

St. Paul says it is God's Spirit that makes us sure we are his children:

> For all who are led by the Spirit of God are sons of God.
> . . . When we cry, "Abba! Father!" it is the Spirit himself
> bearing witness with our spirit that we are children of God.
> —Romans 8:14-16

We call on the Holy Spirit in this hymn to help us live as children of God:

> *Blessed Spirit, who renewest*
> *All that dwell upon the earth,*
> *When the evil one assails us*
> *Help us prove our heavenly birth;*
> *Arm us with thy mighty sword*
> *In the legions of the Lord.*
>
> *Help us keep the faith forever;*
> *Let not Satan, death or shame*
> *Draw us from thee, or deprive us*
> *Of the honor of thy Name.*
> *When the foe would lure us hence,*
> *Be thou, God, our sure defence.*
> —126 SBH

PRAYER

Dear Lord and Savior: I pray that your spirit may live in me and make me yours. Amen. The Lord's Prayer.

219

"... which he poured out upon us richly through Jesus Christ our Savior ..."

Here we are talking about the mercy which God gives us through Christ. When a judge or a king has mercy on a man who has done wrong, he simply forgives the man who has done wrong and lets him go. But God did much more than just forgive us for our sins. He himself made good our wrong; he himself paid the price we should have paid. He gave his own Son to be killed for our sins. The cross stands for many things, and mercy is one of them. The next time you sit in church, take a good look at the cross on the altar. It stands for God's mercy to you and all men. We all have done wrong, but God has had mercy on us and has given us his Son, who takes away our sins if we believe in him.

The Bible tells us in many places of God's great mercy to us:

> But God, who is rich in mercy, out of the great love with which he loved us, even when we were dead through our trespasses, made us alive together with Christ (by grace you have been saved), and raised us up with him, and made us sit with him in the heavenly places in Christ Jesus.
> —Ephesians 2:4-6

This beautiful hymn speaks of the mercy of God:

> *There's a wideness in God's mercy,*
> *Like the wideness of the sea;*
> *There's a kindness in his justice,*
> *Which is more than liberty.*
>
> *There is no place where earth's sorrows*
> *Are more felt than up in heaven;*
> *There is no place where earth's failings*
> *Have such kindly judgment given.*
>
> *For the love of God is broader*
> *Than the measures of man's mind,*
> *And the heart of the Eternal*
> *Is most wonderfully kind.*
> —493 SBH, 256 CSB

PRAYER

Dear Lord Jesus: I thank you for your great mercy to me. Help me to be merciful to others. Amen. The Lord's Prayer.

Thursday   *The Sacrament of Baptism*

"... so that we might be justified by his grace ..."

The Bible tells us that God is love. That is what we would like to believe, and we should believe it. But most of us have a wrong idea of what love is. We think of love as something that looks the other way when we do wrong, and says, "Oh, that's all right. We'll just pretend you didn't do anything bad." If God had that attitude, he would not be an honest God or a truthful God. He cannot act as if we are good when we are not. But just as our father may pay a neighbor for a window that we have broken, because the window has to be paid for, so God gave his Son to pay for our sins so that our debt would be cleared. That makes us "justified," or puts us in good standing. Debts have to be paid—that is the only honest way—and God has done it for us by his love and his grace.

The idea of being justified by Jesus is stated by St. Paul to the Christians in the Greek city of Corinth:

> But you were washed, you were sanctified, you were justified in the name of the Lord Jesus Christ and in the Spirit of our God.
>
> —1 Corinthians 6:11

This hymn tells how we are justified by what Jesus has done for us:

> *He breaks the power of cancelled sin,*
> *He sets the prisoner free;*
> *His Blood can make the foulest clean;*
> *His Blood avails for me.*
>
> *Look unto Him, ye nations; own*
> *Your God, ye fallen race:*
> *Look, and be saved through faith alone,*
> *Be justified by grace.*
>
> —135 CSB

PRAYER

Dear Lord Jesus: I give you thanks for what you have done for me so that I can be a child of God. Amen. The Lord's Prayer.

Friday   *The Sacrament of Baptism*

"... and become heirs in hope of eternal life."

The word "heir" is said like "air." An heir is a person who has something coming to him in the future, like a throne or a large fortune or a big piece of land. Perhaps you will be heir to your father's business or his property when he is old. Because we are Christians, we are heirs, too—we have something to look forward to in the future. We are the children of God, and our Father has promised us the most wonderful thing of all: eternal life with him and a share in his kingdom. That is worth more than any house or land or business or money, because it is a gift that will last forever, and no one can take it away from us.

The Bible tells us in a number of places that Christians are children and heirs of God:

> ... it is the Spirit himself bearing witness with our spirit that we are children of God, and if children, then heirs, heirs of God and fellow heirs with Christ, provided we suffer with him in order that we may also be glorified with him.
> —Romans 8:16-17

In this favorite Advent hymn we Christians are called "heirs of glory" who wait for Christ, the "Bridegroom" of the church:

The watchers on the mountain
  Proclaim the Bridegroom near;
Go meet him as he cometh
  With hallelujahs clear;
The marriage-feast is waiting,
  The gates wide open stand;
Up, up, ye heirs of glory,
  The Bridegroom is at hand!

Our hope and expectation,
  O Jesus, now appear;
Arise, thou Sun so longed for,
  O'er this benighted sphere!
With hearts and hands uplifted,
  We plead, O Lord, to see
The day of earth's redemption
  That brings us unto thee!
  —14 SBH, 13 CSB

PRAYER

Dear Lord Jesus: Help me to live this life as though I expected to inherit a wonderful kingdom in the future. Amen. The Lord's Prayer.

Saturday   *The Sacrament of Baptism*

"The saying is sure."

These words refer to what St. Paul has said about our salvation and our inheriting eternal life: These things are sure; they are "for real," as youngsters say these days. The fact that our salvation is sure has carried many Christians through all sorts of dangerous and trying experiences. It gave the Christians of the first centuries the strength to face death from swords and lions. It gives our missionaries courage to work for Jesus in lonely and dangerous parts of the world. And it can help you and me to live good Christian lives wherever we are, without being afraid.

The life hereafter was a very sure and real thing for St. Paul:

> I have fought the good fight, I have finished the race, I have kept the faith. Henceforth there is laid up for me the crown of righteousness, which the Lord, the righteous judge, will award to me on that Day, and not only to me but also to all who have loved his appearing.
> —2 Timothy 4:7-8

This stirring hymn tells about the early Christians who were sure of their faith and asks God to give us courage to follow their example:

> *A glorious band, the chosen few,*
> *On whom the Spirit came,*
> *Twelve valiant saints, their hope they knew,*
> *And mocked the cross and flame.*
> *They met the tyrant's brandished steel,*
> *The lion's gory mane;*
> *They bowed their necks the death to feel:*
> *Who follows in their train?*
>
> *A noble army, men and boys,*
> *The matron and the maid,*
> *Around the Saviour's throne rejoice*
> *In robes of light arrayed.*
> *They climbed the steep ascent of heaven*
> *Through peril, toil, and pain;*
> *O God, to us may grace be given*
> *To follow in their train!*
> —562 SBH, 383 CSB

PRAYER

Dear Lord Jesus: Make me so sure of my heavenly home that it will give me strength for all the trials and difficulties of this life. Amen. The Lord's Prayer.

223

PART FIVE

The Sacrament of Holy Communion

1

What is Holy Communion?

It is the sacrament instituted by Christ himself,
in which he gives us his body and blood
in and with the bread and wine.

What are the Words of Institution?

Our Lord Jesus Christ, in the night in which he was betrayed,
took bread; and when he had given thanks,
he broke it and gave it to his disciples,
saying, "Take, eat, this is my body,
   which is given for you;
this do in remembrance of me."

After the same manner also he took the cup after supper,
and when he had given thanks,
he gave it to them, saying,
"Drink of it, all of you;
this cup is the new testament in my blood,
which is shed for you, and for many, for the remission of sins;
this do, as often as you drink it, in remembrance of me."

2

What benefits do we receive from this sacrament?

The benefits of this sacrament are
    pointed out by the words,
*given and shed for you for the remission
    of sins.*
These words assure us that in the
    sacrament
we receive forgiveness of sins, life, and
    salvation.
For where there is forgiveness of sins,
there is also life and salvation.

3

How can eating and drinking do all this?

It is not eating and drinking that does
    this,
but the words, *given and shed for you
    for the remission of sins.*
These words, along with eating and
    drinking, are the main thing in the
    sacrament.
And whoever believes these words
has exactly what they say,
    forgiveness of sins.

4

When is a person rightly prepared to receive this sacrament?

Fasting and other outward preparations
    serve a good purpose.
However, that person is well prepared
    and worthy who believes these words,
*given and shed for you for the remission
    of sins.*
But anyone who does not believe these
    words, or doubts them,
is neither prepared nor worthy,
for the words *for you* require simply
    a believing heart.

Sunday   *The Sacrament of Holy Communion*

". . . in which he gives us his body and blood . . ."

We cannot say in one simple sentence just what the Lord's Supper means, because it means several things, all at the same time. The first thing that the Lord's Supper should mean to us is that our Lord gave himself as a sacrifice for our sins. He told his disciples, "This is my body, which is given for you," and ". . . my blood, which is shed for you." People in olden times used to sacrifice oxen and sheep on their altars as presents to their gods so that their sins would be forgiven. But oxen and sheep cannot take away the sins of the world—our sins. So God gave himself as a sacrifice on the cross to pay for the sins of mankind. He gave his body and his blood so that we might be saved.

The New Testament tells us that Jesus' sacrifice for us is worth much more than any other kind:

> For if the sprinkling of defiled persons with the blood of goats and bulls and with the ashes of a heifer sanctifies for the purification of the flesh, how much more shall the blood of Christ, who through the eternal Spirit offered himself without blemish to God, purify your conscience from dead works to serve the living God.
> —Hebrews 9:13-14

In this beautiful children's hymn we sing about how Jesus died to save us:

> *There is a green hill far away,*
> *Without a city wall,*
> *Where the dear Lord was crucified,*
> *Who died to save us all.*
>
> *We may not know, we cannot tell*
> *What pains he had to bear,*
> *But we believe it was for us*
> *He hung and suffered there.*
> —77 SBH, 544 CSB

PRAYER

Dear Lord Jesus: I thank you that you have given yourself as a sacrifice so that I may be saved. Amen. The Lord's Prayer.

Monday   *The Sacrament of Holy Communion*

"... in which he gives us his body and blood ..."

Another thing that the Lord's Supper means is that Christ is really a part of us, and we are a part of him. Jesus once told his disciples, "I am the living bread which came down from heaven; if any one eats of this bread, he will live for ever." Jesus told the woman at the well, "Whoever drinks of the water that I shall give him will never thirst; the water that I shall give him will become in him a spring of water welling up to eternal life." Jesus calls himself the "bread" and "water" of eternal life. Just as we cannot live this life without bread and water, so we cannot have everlasting life without eating the bread and drinking the water which is Christ, without his being a part of us. So in the Lord's Supper we eat and drink Christ, who is the bread and water of life.

Jesus says that in the Lord's Supper or Holy Communion he comes to live in us and we in him:

> He who eats my flesh and drinks my blood abides in me, and I in him.
> —John 6:56

This Holy Communion hymn speaks of Jesus as the bread and water of life:

> *O Bread of life from heaven,*
> *To weary pilgrims given,*
>   *O Manna from above!*
> *The souls that hunger feed thou,*
> *The hearts that seek thee lead thou,*
>   *With thy most sweet and tender love.*
>
> *O fount of grace redeeming,*
> *O river ever streaming*
>   *From Jesus' holy side!*
> *Come thou, thyself bestowing*
> *On thirsting souls, and flowing*
>   *Till all their wants are satisfied.*
> —271 SBH

PRAYER

Dear Lord Jesus: I thank you that you have the power to live in me and that I can live in you. Amen. The Lord's Prayer.

Tuesday   *The Sacrament of Holy Communion*

". . . in which he gives us his body and blood . . ."

There is still a third meaning that the Lord's Supper ought to have for us. On the last evening with his disciples Jesus said to them, "This cup is the new testament in my blood." The word "testament" means a pledge or an agreement. When people long ago wanted to make a very important agreement, they would seal it in blood. Our American Indians made their pledges that way. When Jesus died on the cross he gave his blood for a new testament, or pledge, to us, that if we believe in him he will save us from our sins. So at each Lord's Supper Christ makes this pledge in his blood again to us.

Isaiah, the prophet, who lived hundreds of years before Christ, foretold that Jesus would die for our sins:

> But he was wounded for our transgressions,
> he was bruised for our iniquities;
> upon him was the chastisement that made us whole,
> and with his stripes we are healed.
> —Isaiah 53:5

We sing of Jesus' pledge to us in this communion hymn:

> *Draw nigh and take the Body of the Lord,*
> *And drink the holy Blood for you out-poured.*
>
> *Approach ye then with faithful hearts sincere,*
> *And take the pledges of salvation here.*
> —273 SBH

PRAYER

Dear Lord Jesus: I thank you for your pledge of forgiveness which we receive in Holy Communion. Amen. The Lord's Prayer.

"What is a sacrament?"

We have been thinking about two sacraments: Baptism and the Lord's Supper. It will be easier now for us to understand what the word "sacrament" itself means. As Christians we often talk about spiritual and material things. The spiritual things, like love and forgiveness, cannot be touched or seen or heard. But material things, like bread and water, can be seen and touched. Since we are both spiritual (our minds and souls) and material (our bodies), God has to deal with us in a way that is both spiritual and material. That is why he gave us the sacraments of Baptism and the Lord's Supper. In them we have God's love and his forgiveness of sins, which are spiritual and which we cannot see or touch or hear. But we can see and touch the water, and hear the minister read God's Word in Baptism. In the Lord's Supper we can see and taste the bread and the wine and hear God's Word. Seeing, touching, tasting, and hearing make God's love and forgiveness more real to us and help us to remember them.

Jesus knew that the bread and the wine of the Last Supper would help his disciples remember his love for them:

> "This is my body which is for you. Do this in remembrance of me. . . This cup is the new covenant in my blood. Do this, as often as you drink it, in remembrance of me."
> —1 Corinthians 11:24b and 25b

We tell Jesus in this hymn that the Lord's Supper helps us to remember what he did for us:

> *According to thy gracious word,*
> *In meek humility,*
> *This will I do, my dying Lord,*
> *I will remember thee.*
>
> *Thy Body, broken for my sake,*
> *My bread from heaven shall be;*
> *Thy testamental cup I take,*
> *And thus remember thee.*
> —266 SBH, 191 CSB

PRAYER

Dear Lord Jesus: I thank you for your sacraments, which help me to understand and remember your love for me. Amen. The Lord's Prayer.

Thursday   *The Sacrament of Holy Communion*

". . . given and shed for you for the remission of sins . . ."

There are people who think of the Lord's Supper as a sort of magic. They believe that the bread and the wine have some kind of mysterious power in themselves. But the water of Baptism and the bread and the wine of the Lord's Supper would have no particular meaning at all by themselves. It is the Word of God that goes along with them that gives them meaning and makes them sacraments. Christ tells us that his body and his blood have been "given" and "shed" for our sins. The bread and the wine are there to help us understand and believe those words. God's Word makes the sacrament, and our believing his Word is the only thing that brings us any good from the sacrament. There is nothing automatic or magical about it.

Jesus tells us that God's Word and our faith are what save us:

> Truly, truly, I say to you, he who hears my word and believes him who sent me, has eternal life.
> —John 5:24a

This hymn speaks about the importance of God's Word and our faith in Holy Communion:

> *We hear thine invitation;*
> *We heed, O Lord, thy call;*
> *Thy word of consolation*
> *Is spoken here for all*
> *Who, drawn unto thy loving heart,*
> *Would seek from thee a blessing*
> *Ere from thy side they part.*
>
> *We would be thine forever*
> *To do thy gracious will,*
> *Let naught from thee us sever,*
> *But keep us faithful still.*
> *Here linger with us, Lord, in love,*
> *Till we shall see thy glory*
> *And feast with thee above.*
> —264 SBH

PRAYER

Dear Lord Jesus: I thank you for your Word which gives meaning and power to the sacraments and which tells me of your love for me. Amen. The Lord's Prayer.

Friday   *The Sacrament of Holy Communion*

"When is a person rightly prepared to receive this sacrament?"

Sometimes when the minister asks people why they have not had the Lord's Supper for a long time, they will answer, "I don't feel that I'm good enough." That is the same answer many others give when they are asked why they don't go to church, or why they don't pray. A person who feels that way—that he is not good enough or worthy enough to come to God—is only half right. None of us is worthy enough to come to God, because we have sinned against him. But that is exactly why we should come to the Lord's Supper: because it is for those who have sinned and who confess their sins and who want God's forgiveness. If we thought we were good and did not need forgiveness, then there would be no use coming. All of us have sinned, and we all need forgiveness. And the way we can be worthy of the Lord's Supper is to admit our sins and want to be forgiven.

St. John encourages us to come to God with our sins and ask forgiveness:

> If we say we have no sin, we deceive ourselves, and the truth is not in us. If we confess our sins, he is faithful and just, and will forgive our sins and cleanse us from all unrighteousness.
>
> —1 John 1:8-9

This hymn expresses the kind of thoughts and feelings that make us ready to receive Holy Communion:

> *I have no help but thine; nor do I need*
> *Another arm save thine to lean upon;*
> *It is enough, my Lord, enough indeed;*
> *My strength is in thy might, thy might alone.*
>
> *Mine is the sin, but thine the righteousness;*
> *Mine is the guilt, but thine the cleansing Blood;*
> *Here is my robe, my refuge, and my peace;*
> *Thy Blood, thy righteousness, O Lord, my God.*
> —275 SBH, 183 CSB

PRAYER

Dear Lord Jesus: I thank you that your sacrament was meant for sinners and that you are willing to receive and forgive me. Amen. The Lord's Prayer.

Saturday   *The Sacrament of Holy Communion*

"... given and shed for you ..."

Some time ago we said that if someone asked us what Christianity is all about, we could answer: "God's wanting to bring us back to himself." Another answer we could give would be to point to the Lord's Supper. In the Lord's Supper we act out, in a way we can see and hear and touch, what Christianity is all about. Christianity is about forgiveness. In the bread and wine which we receive at the Lord's Supper we have the body and blood of our Lord as a pledge that our sins have been forgiven. Christianity is about happiness. In the Lord's Supper we are not only promised forgiveness, but also eternal life—so we go away full of happiness and joy.

These words of Jesus show how Holy Communion holds the true meaning of Christianity:

> Jesus said to them, "I am the bread of life; he who comes to me shall not hunger, and he who believes in me shall never thirst . . . he who eats my flesh and drinks my blood has eternal life, and I will raise him up at the last day.
> —John 6:35 and 54

In this hymn we sing about the happiness that we receive from the Lord's Supper and from our Christian faith:

> *Deck thyself with joy and gladness,*
> *Dwell no more, my soul in sadness;*
> *Let the daylight shine upon thee,*
> *Put thy wedding garment on thee,*
> *For the Lord of life unending*
> *Unto thee his call is sending:*
> *Come, for now the King most holy*
> *Stoops to thee in likeness lowly.*
>
> —262 SBH, 182 CSB

PRAYER

Dear Lord Jesus: I thank you for the promise and the joy of my Christian faith. Amen. The Lord's Prayer.

About the Author

Louis E. Ulrich has been the senior pastor at Grace Lutheran Church, Kenosha, Wis., since 1958. He also is a part-time faculty member of Carthage College in Kenosha, teaching the freshman course in Old Testament. Previously he was campus pastor at the University of North Dakota for three years where he taught credit courses in religion. Before this, he served two congregations in Minneapolis, Minn.

Pastor Ulrich received his B.S. degree from the University of Wisconsin in elementary education; his B.D. from Northwestern Lutheran Theological Seminary in Minneapolis; his M.A. from the University of Minnesota in Reformation and Renaissance History. His education orientation has been the chief motivation in writing a devotional book geared to family understanding.

In the summer of 1961 Pastor Ulrich visited the Holy Land as part of a Bible Lands Seminar sponsored by the department of Hebrew and Semitic Studies of the University of Wisconsin. During the trip he took more than 700 colored slides on Bible background, and has organized a series of lectures around this material.

He is a past president of the Minnesota Sunday School association and serves as a "key" pastor in the long range parish education program of Lutheran Church in America. He has written several articles for parish education periodicals as well as devotions for the *Light for To-Day, Upper Room* and *The Word in Season* devotional booklets.

Before entering the Seminary, he served with the Army Corps of Engineers for five years, rising from enlisted man to captain. He and Mrs. Ulrich are the parents of five children.